A Rhythm of Prayer

A Rhythm of Prayer

A COLLECTION OF MEDITATIONS

FOR RENEWAL

Edited by Sarah Bessey

CONVERGENT

NEW YORK

Compilation, Introduction, "A Reminder,"
"A Prayer to Breathe," "A Prayer for When You Don't
Even Know What You Want," "A Prayer to Learn
to Love the World Again," "A Centering Practice for Prayer,"
"Instructions for an Evening of Your Life," and
"A Benediction" copyright © 2021 by Sarah Bessey

Published in the United States by Convergent Books,
an imprint of Random House, a division of
Penguin Random House LLC, New York.

CONVERGENT BOOKS is a registered trademark
and its C colophon is a trademark of
Penguin Random House LLC.

LIBRARY OF CONGRESS CATALOGING-IN-PUBLICATION DATA
NAMES: Bessey, Sarah, editor.
TITLE: A rhythm of prayer / edited by Sarah Bessey.
DESCRIPTION: First edition. | New York : Convergent, 2020.
IDENTIFIERS: LCCN 2020016626 (print) | LCCN 2020016627 (ebook) |
ISBN 9780593137215 (hardcover) | ISBN 9780593137222 (ebook)
SUBJECTS: LCSH: Prayers. | Christian women—Religious life.
CLASSIFICATION: LCC BV260 .R49 2020 (print) | LCC BV260 (ebook) |
DDC 242/.843—dc23
LC record available at https://lccn.loc.gov/2020016626
LC ebook record available at https://lccn.loc.gov/2020016627

Printed in the United States of America on acid-free paper

convergentbooks.com

98765432

Book design by Barbara M. Bachman

FOR RACHEL HELD EVANS:

Who gave permission to a generation,
Who made origami out of hate mail,
Who kept the faith,
Who told the truth,
Who dared to wonder "What if I'm wrong?"
    out loud,
Who was willing to keep wrestling until
    the blessing came,
Who pulled up more chairs to the Table and
    scooted over to make room,
Who made us laugh and made us think,
Who was bold and courageous and kind,
Who would not be budged from her conviction
    that this Gospel is Good News for everyone,
Who moved to the margins because she knew
    this is the centre of God's Story,
Who never lost her love for telling that Story,
Who loved us,
And whom we loved.
Eshet chayil, *woman of valour.*
1981–2019

I am writing because sometimes
we are closer to the truth in our vulnerability
than in our safe certainties.

—RACHEL HELD EVANS

. . .

EDITOR'S NOTE:
This is also part of
why we are praying.

CONTENTS

. . .

PART TWO
DISORIENTATION

———

PART THREE

REORIENTATION

by Sarah Bessey

I GREW UP AND CAME OF AGE IN PRAYER CIRCLES, particularly prayer circles with women. In living rooms and the basements of churches, the women of my life—from church mothers to brand-new babies yawning in footie sleepers to earnest youth group leaders—would gather to pray together. We prayed so differently—there was the lady who prayed exclusively with words from scripture, one who prayed like she was preaching, one who told everyone off in her prayers, another who cried throughout. We spoke in tongues and in silence; we read prayers from other people and made up our own. Sometimes we simply sat together, in the quiet, hands open and waiting like Quakers for the Spirit to move in or through one of us. We prayed for the world, for justice, for the poor, for our nation, and for each other, but we also learned to just sit with Jesus together.

I miss those prayer circles. I miss the feeling of being encircled in homemade prayer with others. Given the nature of my work as both a writer and in co-leading the

Evolving Faith community, I hear from people all the time that they don't know how to pray anymore, that they miss prayer, or that perhaps they, too, need to re-imagine prayer.

And so I began to dream of this book. A book that could co-create that space for those of us who wander in the wilderness more often than not—an open circle where you could pull up a chair and find rest in the prayers of those who also walk with God.

Often when we find ourselves at a crossroad in our faith, rethinking everything from church to scripture to family to art to politics to science to prayer, we think we have only two options: double down or burn it down. So when it comes to prayer, we might mistakenly believe that if we can't pray the way we used to or the way we were taught, somehow that means we can't or don't pray anymore, period.

Many of us were introduced to prayer in one particular way, largely depending on our culture, our religion, our faith tradition, our family. And many of us have lost those old pathways of prayer. There are many reasons for this: perhaps the tradition we inherited was never one we felt comfortable with; perhaps the prayer warrior who once took us under their wing somewhere along the way lost our trust, or any number of good and valid reasons. This can leave us in a disorienting season emptied of prayer, longing for prayer, yet not knowing how to begin again. Sometimes when we lose prayer, it can be for the best: now that we no longer pray as we were taught, we are finally able to pray in both old and new words and silences.

When I first began to envision this book about prayer, I knew right away what I *didn't* want to give you: a nice and tidy new set of prayers to co-opt for your own. Nope, what I wanted was equal parts example and invitation, permission and challenge, to acknowledge the heaviness of our grief and at the same time broaden our hope.

Frankly, I love to pray, and I think the prayers of people like us—however we show up to these pages—matter. Not in spite of scripture but because of it. Not in spite of Church but because of her. Not in spite of our questions and doubts but because of them. Not in spite of our grief and our longing, our yearning for justice and our anger, but because of them.

So no, the point of this is not to give you prayers to pray but to show you: you still get to pray. Prayer is still for you. You still get to cry out to God, you still get to yell, weep, praise, and sit in the silence until you sink down into the Love of God that has always been holding you whether you knew it or not.

I want this to help you feel a bit less alone. My hope is that you'll borrow language from these prayers and be reminded that you are held—always, fully, completely—in the Love of God. I want this to be an act of resistance at this moment in our time, a way for us to fling wide the doors to prayer, to set up a few tables in your wilderness so that we can feast together on truth, justice, and goodness.

So clearly my expectations are very reasonable.

If there is one thing I know about navigating an evolving faith, both through my firsthand experiences and through shepherding many others in this path of wilderness formation, it is this: the work of reclaiming and reimagining is good, hard, holy work.

And it's worthwhile.

There is room for your whole self in prayer. You can bring your whole body to this altar, this place where you meet with God with words or with wordless knowing. You don't need to pretend you aren't angry, that you aren't cynical or afraid, that you aren't feeling a bit hopeless or uncomfortable or envious or tired. That's how a lot of the Psalms came to be, after all. I believe that scripture gives us a more fulsome and complete view of prayer than we were perhaps taught and so I wanted this book to show all of them.

In these pages, we have liturgy and guided meditations; we also have laments and even some imprecatory prayers, which may make you uncomfortable with their honesty. We have thanksgiving and praise, we have cries for justice, challenge, and comfort, we have practices and psalms. I'm from a Pentecostal, charismatic background myself, and so I am all the way here for the naming and calling out of what Paul called "powers and principalities" because in these days I don't know what else to call evils like white supremacy, patriarchy, homophobia, nationalism, colonialism, transphobia, racism. Name them for what they are, Church, and let's take it to prayer, especially as we take it to the streets.

You may sense the invitation of the Holy Spirit to lean into new language, new practices, old longings. That's okay. I ask only that you stay open to the possibility of healing, to the possibility of hope, of renewal and restoration, perhaps even resurrection, through prayer.

It is in prayer that I have most encountered the wild and inclusive, beautiful and welcoming, abundant love of God without filter or measure, without condition or boundary. Prayers like these are one way that our places of weakness become pillars of strength. We bring our whole self to God and find Love was our home all along. That's where we find that our desert will bloom with flowers, the rivers will run again, everything will be redeemed.

I asked each of these women to join this prayer circle because they are my own teachers. In their own lives, they are engaged in speaking prophetically, embodying a challenge to the Empire, exploring new paths of faithfulness, and are rooted in doing justice, loving mercy, and walking humbly with God, in a way that invites and expands our ideas of prayer and God. This community of leaders are speaking to all of the ways we pray—with silence, with our bodies, with ancient prayers, liturgy, rage, swearing, adoration, confession, repentance, demands, yearnings, grief, and all in between. And in this book, they do just that, by giving us a glimpse of their innermost intimate prayers. I pray that we can receive their offerings with gratitude, looking for the invitation from God within each line.

My hope is that you will have your understanding of prayer expanded, lit up, renewed. May these pages encourage you to reengage with prayer, particularly on the other side of a faith shift or sea change. In these pages, may you find a new way to pray, a new way of understanding the ancient ways, and be given a new language to express your own deepest longings and hopes not only for yourself but for the world.

Ultimately, I hope this feels like what those Wednesday night prayer meetings used to be for me: a rhythm of prayer, in all the ways we pray for all the rhythms of our lives. May it be hope for the grieving, tenderness for the hurting, challenge for the comfortable, a kick in the ass for the lethargic, a permission slip allowing rest for the overwhelmed, an anointing for the work ahead, and a sanctuary. It is a way for us to gather together in prayer as we scatter back out into the world at this moment in time.

May you feel at your darkest hour, when you are tired, that God is holding you tight. May you find a new rhythm of prayer that makes you sway, makes you kneel, makes you dance. May you be blessed with discomfort, wonder, and curiosity about the Story with which we all continue to wrestle. May you be quieted by this love, may your striving and hustling pause for a moment so you can know Love is with you; Love is mighty to save; Love is your home. May you experience the surprising, open-door, generous, invitational, creative, disruptive, welcoming Love of God and may you leave these pages filled with unexpected hope.

ASH WEDNESDAY 2020

Orientation

A PRAYER AGAINST EFFICIENCY

...

by Micha Boyett

OH GOD BEYOND TIME, BEYOND THE NUMBER LINE, the hourglass. Beyond moons that wax and wane and waves that push and pull along our fragile ground. Oh God beyond days and weeks and months, God uncontained by our twenty-four hours, free of our borders and yet still within them.

God who is here. God of the meetings, the emails, the PTA, the neck ache, the child crying over homework, the car leaking oil, the head lice, and the sheets to wash. Oh God of the groceries and the knife against the butcher block moving slow across the cucumber. God of the sun's path across a sky we cannot reach. God of midday, God of afternoons and the laughter of children, the clap of a ball on concrete. God of evening color and the muted spread of light in the clouds as the night leaks in. God in the hand I hold, God of the one I love.

God beyond time, we come to you pulled by the bullet points in our calendars, by the titles we keep beside our names, by the goals we've charted and the accomplishments we list to define our value. You see each image we upload to our pocket screens: altered, filtered, and pinned to virtual walls. You, God, touch our distortions and soothe the edges of our efficiency, and only you can make us real.

God beyond the boxes we build to contain our lives, the hours we track and tally. God outside of time, yet here: Come to us, relieve our ragged breaths, slow our steps, relax the red lines that spike in our brains. Tell us what is true. Show us how time rolls like calm water, let us cup it quiet in our hands.

God, teach us to pause in this moment, to tuck ourselves into the curve of your slow arm, that we may know the miracle of now, the gift of this moment: you beside and beyond us, welcoming us outside of all we measure, and standing with us in it. May we see the goodness of our still hours and days, sunrises, sunsets, and the darkness where our rest is found.

Order us, that we may stand within time holding your hand. That we may know we are enough, not because of what we make of these hours, but because within these hours—with you—we are being made.

MICHA BOYETT is the author of *Found: A Story of Questions, Grace, and Everyday Prayer,* and one of the hosts of *The Lucky Few* podcast, a weekly podcast celebrating the lives of people with Down syndrome. She writes about ancient Christian spiritual practices, disability, and the life of faith. Boyett holds an MFA in poetry from Syracuse University and has written for *The Washington Post, Christianity Today, Patheos,* and various other publications. She lives in San Francisco with her husband and their three sons.

Why must people kneel down to pray? If I really wanted to pray I'll tell you what I'd do. I'd go out into a great big field all alone or in the deep, deep woods, and I'd look up into the sky— up—up—up—into that lovely blue sky that looks as if there was no end to its blueness. And then I'd just feel *a prayer.*

—L. M. MONTGOMERY,
Anne of Green Gables

SHE SAID, "HOW DO YOU KNOW WHEN YOU ARE HEARING FROM GOD?"

. . .

by Amena Brown

She said, "How do you know when you are
    hearing from God?"
I didn't know how to explain
It is to explain the butter grit of cornbread
    to a mouth that just discovered it has a
    tongue
The sound of jazz to ears that only ever thought
    they'd be lobes of flesh
The sight of sunsets to blinded eyes that in
    an instant can see
To fail at the ability to give words to how the scent
    of baked bread can make the mind recall a
    memory
Every detail
Of a house, a room, a kitchen, a conversation
Like explaining to a newborn baby this is what it
    feels like to be held
My words never felt so small, so useless,
    so incapable

I wanted to say
Put your hand in the middle of your chest
Feel the rhythm there
I wanted to say you will find the holy text in so
    many places
On crinkly pages of scripture
In dusty hymnals
In the creases of a grandmother's smile
The way she clasps her hands
The way she prays familiar, with reverence as if to
    dignitary and friend
The way she sings a simple song from her spirit
    and porches turn to cathedrals

I learned from my great-grandmother how to
    pray
How to talk to God
How to listen
Watching her and the other silver-haired church
    mothers gather in her living room
Worn wrinkled hands on top of leather bibles
    well traveled

They prayed living room prayers because you
    don't have to be inside the four walls of a
    church to cry out to the God who made you
Because no matter where you sing or scream or
    whisper God's ears can hear you

And despite what the laws say or what our
    human flaws say
God's ears don't play favorites
God's ears don't assess bank accounts or social
    status before they attune themselves to the
    story your tears or your fears are telling

God's ears are here for the babies
For the immigrant, for the refugee
For the depressed, for the lonely
For the dreamers
The widow, the orphan
The oppressed and the helpless
Those about to make a mess or caught in the
    middle of cleaning one up
Dirt don't scare God's ears
God is a gardener
God knows things can't grow without sun, rain,
    and soil

I want to tell her to hear God
You have to be willing to experience what's holy
    in places many people don't deem to be sacred
That sometimes God sits next to you on a barstool
Spilling truth to you like too many beers
That God knows very well the dance we'll do
When we love ourselves so little that just about
    anyone will do

That God cares about the moments we find our-
    selves
On the edge of a cliff
On the edge of sanity
On the edge of society
Even when we have less than an inch left of the
    thread that's been holding us together

I want to tell her God is always waiting
Lingering after the doors close
And the phone doesn't ring
And we are finally alone
God is always saying
I love you
I am here
Don't go, stay
Please

I try to explain how God is pleading with us
To trust
To love
To listen
That God's voice is melody and bass lines and
    whisper and thunder and grace

Sometimes when I pray, I think of her
How the voice of God was lingering in her very
    question

How so many of us just like her
Just like me
Just like you
Are still searching
Still questioning, still doubting
I know I don't have all the answers
I know I never will
That sometimes the best thing we can do is put our
    hands in the middle of our chest
Feel the rhythm there
Turn down the noise in our minds, in our lives
And whisper,
God
Whatever you want to say
I'm here
I'm listening

AMENA BROWN is a spoken word poet, performing artist, and event host whose work interweaves keep-it-real storytelling, rhyme, and humor. The author of five spoken word albums and two nonfiction books, Amena wrote and collaborated with award-winning actress, producer, and activist Tracee Ellis Ross on the Manifesta and Glossary for Ross's natural hair product line, PATTERN. She's also the host of *HER with Amena Brown* podcast, which centers and elevates the stories and experiences of Black, Indigenous, Latinx, and Asian women. Amena lives in Atlanta, Georgia, with her husband, DJ Opdiggy.

A PSALM OF
POSSIBILITY

...

by Rev. Gail Song Bantum

For all those who are confronted by seeming
boundaries, limitations, and impossibilities, this is
a psalm reminding us of who God is—in God's
wholly otherness and God's holy withness.

God
Creator, Hoverer
You speak and we form
You breathe life and we awake
You said "it is good" and we believe
God
The Red Sea before us, shouting impossibility
They say we can't, we shouldn't, and we wouldn't
Words seeded from our youth, the limits and
    the lies
There must be truer truths in us to confound,
    resist, defy
Created from nothing, said something,
    made everything
This God

The Lord will fight for us, so we need only
  to be still
Still our soul, stand out loud, trusting that God is
El Roi, God who sees, bears witness to a name
At her sound, ____ leaps, demands possibility
Immanuel, God with us, for us, within us
God
You said "it is good" and we believe
You breathe life and we awake
You speak and we form
Creator, Hoverer
God

Rev. Gail Song Bantum is the lead pastor of Quest Church in Seattle, Washington. Having worked in pastoral ministry for over twenty years, she is particularly passionate about empowering and developing leaders and has launched multiple mentoring cohorts specifically for WoC leaders and pastors. Rev. Bantum is a sought-after speaker and leader, having previously served as president of the ECC North American Asian Pastors Association as well as a board member of the Seattle School of Theology & Psychology. She is an ordained minister and received her M.Div. from Duke Divinity School. Rev. Bantum; her husband, Dr. Brian Bantum; and their three sons reside in Seattle.

God, please help me not be an asshole, is about as common a prayer as I pray in my life.

—REV. NADIA BOLZ-WEBER

GOD OF COMPASSION

. . .

by Rev. Nadia Bolz-Weber

[Jesus] went to a town called Nain, and his disciples and a large crowd went with him. As he approached the town, a man who had died was being carried out. He was his mother's only son, and she was a widow; and with her was a large crowd from the town. When the Lord saw her, he had compassion for her. He came forward and touched the bier, and the bearers stood still. And he said, "Young man, I say to you, rise!" The dead man sat up and began to speak, and Jesus gave him to his mother.

—LUKE 7:11–15 NRSV

GOD OF COMPASSION,

As you did in Nain, enter *our* city gates. Enter into the somber roads down which our hearses drive and the glad streets down which our children run. Enter the parks where the junkies shoot up and the yuppies listen to jazz. Walk uninvited into starter mansions and cheap motel rooms that charge by the hour. Stroll into the cool-air freezer section where the pregnant women escape the heat and the bus stop benches where the weary wait. Enter every law office and adult bookstore. Step into the spaces we say we feel your awesomeness *and* the places where we claim your forsakenness. Enter our city gates, God of Compassion, as you did the city of Nain. And bless.

Bless the things we mistakenly think are already dead. Bless that which we have already begun to carry out of town to bury. Bless our rocky marriages and our college-age kids who smoke too much pot. Bless the person at work whom we love to hate. Bless the chronically sick. Bless the one who has no one. Bless what we call insignificant and which you call magnificent. Bless it all and love what only you can love: the ugly, abandoned, and unsanitary in the wash of humanity upon which you have nothing but a gleaming compassion—when we have none.

God of Compassion who saw the widow of Nain, we thank you for seeing us. For seeing our loneliness and our bravery. For seeing the times we can't say what we need to. For seeing the ones who have never felt like they are enough, but whom you know already are and always have been. For seeing the moments when we are more than we thought we could be. For seeing what no one else can or will. Thank you for seeing as beautiful what we call ugly. In your compassion, teach us to see each other.

Reach out and raise us, God of Compassion. Touch us as you did the wood on which the widow's son lay and speak those same words to us: *Young man, arise.* Little girl, get up. To we who think we are not worthy to be loved and medicate ourselves with food and booze and shopping, say "rise up." To we who have been hurt by those who say they follow you, say "rise up." To those who feel unworthy of forgiveness, say "rise up." To the ones who care for the least of these and who feel too burnt-out to keep going, say "rise up." To we who are holding on to resentments like a security blanket, say "rise up." To those who hide their failings behind their good works, say "rise up." To the unloved child who has no idea that one day they will change the world, say "rise up."

And when again, God of Compassion, you have raised the dead—when again you have made whole that which is broken, when again you have reached into the graves we dig ourselves and loved us back to life—don't stop there. Like the young man of Nain, help us to sit up and speak. Give us words that are not empty affirmation, but give us strong words, as real as the very soil from which you raised us.

Give us the words, Lord, but also give us the pause before the words. Please.

And then, as you did the son to his mother, give us one to another. Make us one in this fractured world.

And help us to know that when we do not have enough compassion for the road ahead, that you do, and that is enough.

Amen.

REV. NADIA BOLZ-WEBER first hit the *New York Times* list with her 2013 memoir—the bitingly honest and inspiring *Pastrix*—followed by the critically acclaimed *New York Times* bestseller *Accidental Saints* in 2015, and *Shameless* in 2019. A former stand-up comic and a recovering alcoholic, Bolz-Weber is the founder and former pastor of a Lutheran congregation in Denver, House for All Sinners and Saints, and currently speaks at colleges and conferences around the globe. She is the host of *The Confessional with Nadia Bolz-Weber* podcast, in association with The Moth.

When two of you get together
on anything at all on earth
and make a prayer of it,
my Father in heaven goes into
action. And when two or three of
you are together because of me,
you can be sure that I'll be there.

—MATTHEW 18:19–20 MSG

MY MEMORY OF
THEIR PRAYERS

...

by Rev. Winnie Varghese

WHEN MY GRANDMOTHER DIED, LOTS OF PEOPLE came by that we didn't know. Many were part of the women's prayer meeting in her neighborhood. One of the members was a four-year-old girl who attended the prayer meetings with her mother. She had adopted my grandmother as a special friend and insisted upon visiting when my grandmother became bedridden. One morning, the little girl got up, dressed herself, and walked herself the few blocks over to my grandmother's house. It wasn't until later that day that her worried father found her, after my aunt called to report that his daughter had arrived alone. There she was, sitting next to my grandmother, holding her hand and chatting. When her father arrived, the young girl was confused why anyone was surprised she would have made the trip herself. Her friend needed her.

MY MOTHER WILL OCCASIONALLY call and text me with a name and a concern, and tell me to pray for the person.

Usually it's someone I've not met paired with a scary diagnosis. I do the same with her, often for myself when I am worried. It feels like a solid handoff to me. If it's in Mommy's hands, I can let it be, for now.

For the record, I'm not really that kind of Christian. I like a chanted service, incense, and a script.

But when the absolute bottom falls out of my capacity to cope, I ask my mother to pray for me, and I know my parents will—during their evening prayer on the sofa, in detail. These days when I pray, I send all of my hopes and fears into the air over the Hudson River, trying to remain long enough for the language of praise to come to me naturally. The words eventually come, usually in the form of an old song from my childhood.

Nothing feels steady around me anymore. I don't know if it is about the horrors of this political moment, or the kind of work I am doing, or my age. I really don't know. In my work at times it feels like the weight of inequity, the power of the state over vulnerable people, are close, wicked, terrifying. The fragility of the bodies broken by it, present. The hauntedness of this land, the generations of abuse and exploitation, palpable.

I have been praying to discern, to have courage and clarity amid all this. I pray for the sense of purpose of that four-year-old.

When I pray, I remember the Friday evening prayer meetings of my childhood, when the prayers, songs, and words were spoken in Malayalam. I wonder how much of my spirituality was formed by a language I barely understood.

Spaces like this taught me liturgy and music. For us kids, we couldn't understand the words, just the emotions. The aunties and uncles would settle into their seats and take off their glasses, anticipating tears. I never wondered back then why they were crying.

Now that I'm closer to the age they were then, I wonder:

Had they made mistakes?

Did they have regrets?

Was someone sick?

Did they miss someone far away?

What were they telling God and one another in prayer?

Did we do it?

Were we all very sad?

I couldn't tell you today what was being said in those living rooms in the 1980s, but I can tell you that after decades of resistance, my prayers today are much like my memory of their prayers.

When I stay in prayer long enough, I am surprised by the level of emotion I inevitably encounter within myself. The stillness brings the weight, the sadness, and the freedom it always has, and a profound sense for me of what is true.

"Enthathisayame daivathin sneham . . ."—"How magnificent or wondrous is God's love; who can fathom it"—when we were kids, songs like this guided us

through an entire cycle of emotional possibilities in just a few hours. We finished these prayer meetings with an hour of excellent emotional eating of good Indian food together. We did this once a week, even though our parents must have been so tired from the work of the past week and weekend to come. These prayer meetings were a touchstone of where we had come from and what could become of us. They functioned as a passing on of a particular practice of Christianity, but with no teaching of doctrine or even concern that we did not speak the language. A profound formation that I remember as a swirling of all of those realities in the language and melody they came in, left imprinted on our hearts as feelings, feelings safely shared when God had gathered us and bid our praise.

THE REV. WINNIE VARGHESE is an Episcopal priest at Trinity Church Wall Street. Before coming to Trinity, Rev. Varghese was the rector of St. Mark's in the Bowery, a historic Episcopal congregation in New York City. From 2003 to 2009, she served as the Episcopal Chaplain at Columbia University. She is a blogger for Patheos, author of *Church Meets World*, editor of *What We Shall Become*, and author of numerous articles and chapters on social justice and the church.

A REMINDER

...

by Sarah Bessey

*Y*OU DON'T HAVE TO BE PRODUCTIVE AND YOU DON'T have to change the world. You're already so loved.

You don't have to be smart. You don't have to be simple. You don't have to read all the right books by the right people. You're already so loved.

You don't have to be beautiful and thin with an articulated and ironic fashion sense, not at all. But if you're into that kind of thing, well, that's okay, too. You don't have to be healthy in your mind or in your body. You don't have to be in full-time vocational ministry. You can watch horrible television or you can be proud of your televisionless home. You can be artistic or scientific. You can spend your life travelling to meet beautiful people or you can live and die in the town where you were born.

You don't have to conform to someone else's ideas of holy or acceptable. You can be from the wrong side of the tracks or the gated community, suburbs or urban or rural. You can work with your hands and your mind, your back and your brain. You don't have to be educated, not at all. You don't have to have a degree or letters after your name. You don't have to know the right people and boast a carefully curated Instagram feed with the famous and the beautiful and the influential. You don't have to be conservative and you don't have to be liberal. You don't have to identify with certain political persuasions or ideology on sexuality or science or socioeconomics or foreign policy. You can be a social justice warrior or, you know, not.

None of that moves the metre of your belovedness. God won't say, *Okay, now I love her just a bit more because, look, she is finally out of debt or thin or powerful or influential or tireless.*

Your family story can be beautiful or terrible—or, like most of us, a bit of both. Perhaps you're famous or well-known or influential, that's okay. Perhaps you are quiet and unknown, maybe you hate that, maybe you love it. You don't have to be a mother or a father, you don't have to be married, you don't have to be single, you don't have to want children or raise children. You don't have to be sober or clean. You don't have to give away everything you own and take a vow of poverty, you don't have to be prosperous either. Church or no church or a certain kind of church only, whatever.

You can doubt or feel great certainty (even if that certainty is in your doubt). You can believe in God, doubt God, seek God. You can be someone well acquainted with unanswered prayers. You can carry chronic pain or dance through life. You can be introverted or extroverted. You don't have to love yourself or even like yourself, you are loved. Whether your life looks well put together from the outside while hiding a hot mess inside or vice versa, sometimes on the same day, you are loved. Morning lark, night owl, sinner, saint, child of God, siblings all of us, we are loved.

You have nothing to prove. You have nothing to earn.

Sure, any one of those things might change because you are loved. You may know already where God wants to breathe change and wholeness into you, bringing your life more into line with the person you were meant to be all along.

Love can and does and will transform us in every way—our ideology, our opinions, our habits, our values, our priorities, our very names. But it's not a prerequisite or a requirement, it's not behavior modification, it never is, not for Love.

Love has happened and it is happening and it will happen. It is kind and patient towards you.

You're already so loved, you aren't earning a breath of love or tenderness more than what you already have just by breathing—just by existing, just by being here in the wonder. Your name is already written in the lines of the hands of the universe. You're star-breath-of-dust, and you are beloved, intimately, faithfully, wholly. It's your lifelong rock. You are known. You are loved with delight and abundance, with choice and desire, with covenantal love.

You may feel it or not.

YOU ARE SO LOVED.
You are so loved.
You are so loved.

God is sheer mercy and grace;
Not easily angered, he's rich in love.
He doesn't endlessly nag and scold,
Nor hold grudges forever.
He doesn't treat us as our sins deserve.
Nor pay us back in full for our wrongs.

—PSALM 103:8–10 MSG

A LITURGY OF LONGING

. . .

by Rev. Sandra Maria Van Opstal

Injustice anywhere is a threat to justice everywhere. We are caught in an inescapable network of mutuality, tied in a single garment of destiny. Whatever affects one directly affects all indirectly.

For some strange reason, I can never be what I ought to be until you are what you ought to be. This is the way God's universe is made; this is the way it is structured.

—DR. MARTIN LUTHER KING, JR.

How long, Lord?
How long must we cry out?
How long must the vulnerable sit silent as bombs,
    guns, cages, natural disasters threaten lives?
How long must we hear the agonizing silence of so
    many in the church?
How long, Lord?

Are you listening? Yes? You do! You do? You do
　　see us! You do hear us!

(insert time to ugly cry)

We believe you are at work bringing peace. True
　　peace—flourishing, wholeness, and
well-being. We hear your words of truth and
　　know in our minds that you are:
Lord, the God of gods and Lord of lords, the great
　　God, mighty and awesome.
You show no partiality.
You defend the cause of the fatherless, motherless,
　　and the widow.
You love the stranger.

We believe and we feel overwhelmed—sometimes
　　it is hard to believe that you actually care about
　　the injustice and suffering. When we don't see
　　your work. When we sense the apathy from
　　the church. When we feel small and forget that
　　we were designed to be different and make
　　things different.

When we feel overwhelmed by darkness in the
　　world—the violence, injustice, poverty, op-
　　pression, abuse.
Give us hope not to be overcome.

Give us eyes to see your goodness for our world.
Give us the strength to hold the pain of injustice in
    our world and faith that it will end.
Give us courage to be honest with ourselves about
    why and how we are doing justice.

We believe. *So.* Empower us to disrupt our broken
    thinking by learning *truth* from diverse leaders.
    Enable us to discover the *beauty* of justice and
    inspire action in others. Embolden us to display
    your *goodness* in the world.

Sisters, let us walk in solidarity and mutuality.
Not ignoring distinctives but embracing them.
Not loving beyond our differences but loving
    because of our differences.
Recognizing that differences can inform and
    transform us.
Inviting each of our narratives to contribute to
    what can be.

Sisters, let us act in creativity to rebuild a
    just world.
Where those fleeing danger can find rest.
Where children are not discarded because they do
    not look like us.
Where mothers are not standing over the graves
    of their sons and daughters.

Where violence does not define us and death does
not have the last word.

Jesus, we repent and return to you. As you call us
in Amos 4–5. We hear your call:
Return to me.
Return to me and seek me.
Return to me, seek me, and do justice.
Jesus, we repent, Confessing—
Our complicity in evil systems
Our apathy towards pain
Our pure enjoyment of things that satisfy us
Our inability to forgive just as Christ has
forgiven us.
Thank you for being born as a refugee into a tiny
ethnic minority, oppressed and persecuted to
death by the empire, and yet never fighting
back in the form of empire but embodying
self-sacrificing resistance.

Jesus, You came to proclaim good news to the
poor by proclaiming freedom for the prisoners
and recovery of sight for the blind. You came
not only proclaiming freedom but freeing the
oppressed. We know that we can be agents of
justice but only you can liberate. We pray,
we engage, we do our work, but only you
bring salvation, You bring healing, you bring

liberation. Only your power can stand against the darkness.

Call us, repairer of broken walls and restorer of Streets with Dwellings. Help us to live justly, to love mercy, and to walk humbly with you, God. Empower us to let justice roll on like a river, righteousness like a never-failing stream!

What does the Lord require of you, but to do justice, love mercy and to walk humbly with God.

—MICAH 6:8

REV. SANDRA MARIA VAN OPSTAL is a pastor, liturgist, and activist. She is the founding director of Chasing Justice, which seeks to guide people to see God's goodness for our world.

Meanwhile, the moment we get tired in the waiting, God's Spirit is right alongside helping us along.

> If we don't know how or what to pray,
> it doesn't matter. He does our praying
> in and for us, making prayer out of our
> wordless sighs, our aching groans.
> He knows us far better than we know
> ourselves, knows our pregnant condition,
> and keeps us present before God. That's
> why we can be so sure that every detail in
> our lives of love for God is worked into
> something good.
>
> —ROMANS 8:26–28 MSG

THIS IS HOW WE'LL MAKE IT

. . .

by Rev. Mihee Kim-Kort

To clasp the hands in prayer is the beginning of
an uprising against the disorder of the world.

—KARL BARTH

*I*T'S GRAY AND WET TODAY. LIKE A SPRING DAY CLOS-
ing the books on a long winter. It's warm out—too
balmy to be winter, yet somehow it's January. Outside,
small green leaves bloom on trees and crocuses push up
through remnants of snow.

But the cathartic relief that usually accompanies these
early hints of warmth evades me. Instead, these days feel
weighty and somber, lonely and dark. Online, post after
post is something about war and terror in the various
countries, families being torn apart at numerous borders, environmental disasters, something about women
being incarcerated or killed, something about guns and
violence and hunger. I wonder, *Where is the light of
Christmas, the wonder and magic of Epiphany? Gone so*

soon . . . ? I want to crawl back into bed and hide under the covers until spring.

When the children were in preschool, we would sing songs every morning in the car. We'd sing the days of the week—"There's Sunday and there's Monday . . ." all the way through to Saturday—to the tune of "The Addams Family." Instead of snapping our fingers we'd click our tongues. Sometimes the song of the day would be "Rise and Shine," or old familiar spirituals like "Deep and Wide" and "I've Got a River of Life." Sometimes the kids sang their own songs—ones they learned from Gan Shalom—the preschool at the local synagogue in town—about Baby Beluga and Shabbat blessings.

They'd also ask us to sing the ones that punctuate our Sunday worship services, too. The Kyrie. The Gloria Patri. The Doxology. The Sanctus during communion. The kids and I would sing each one on the way to school. Over and over.

> "Lord have mercy upon us. Christ have mercy upon us. Lord have mercy upon us."

I'd sing these words, clutching the wheel for dear life like anxious hands clasped in prayer, desperation alive in my voice. When we finished singing, the kids would lead us into the songs that praise and "Sing Hosanna" and acknowledge that heaven and earth are full of God's glory.

But the aching request of the Kyrie would always stay with me throughout the day.

It stays with me still today, an uncomplicated melody that accompanies me and comforts me like the flowers that fall out of my books and notebooks. No matter how small or minute, Anna insists on putting them in there to surprise me—leaves brittle and roots dangling. To remind me. That light and life are always present.

The Kyrie sometimes feels like a protest chant—its persistent roots hanging off, reminding me of the life that anchored it to the soil, words that live always on the edge of winter and spring. Because even as we sing these words, calling for mercy, we do so with the hope and belief that God's mercy is already there.

So, I keep going. I roll out of bed and land on my knees. Push myself up. Keep putting one foot in front of the other and do the sanctified work that is breathing. And I keep looking. Keep seeing. Keep feeling. Keep trying to love like there's no tomorrow. Love hard; love recklessly. Hug a little longer. Play those irrational and illogical games with the twins. Read that board book with Ozzie for the 917th time. Try to answer Andy's question about the schedule for the fifteenth time without exasperation. Let bath time be like a baptism each night, and let the sweat that rolls off my face after a long run be an anointing. Laugh, cook, drink, clean, make a huge mess, sit and stare out the window. Let all of it mean *something*—gratitude, earnestness, hope; let it mean that life is abundant. And tell the children stories about this abundant life—how it's meant to be shared, how it's meant to be experienced by every single human being—even if it means we might have to tell the stories that are sad and hard. Because those are the ones that will shape their empathy and compassion. All of it. All of it is necessary for life right now.

All this work is worship, and it's how we'll make it.

> *Heart of my own heart,*
> *be my sight*
> *by my song*
> *by my light.*
> *Soften my heart that it would break for*
>   *your world,*
> *lead my hands and feet to do work that is*
>   *poured out for the sake of your children,*
> *make me brave, make me hope, make me trust,*
>   *make me love.*
> *In Jesus's sweet, sweet name, amen.*

MIHEE KIM-KORT is a Presbyterian minister, speaker, writer, and slinger of hopeful stories about faith and church. Her writing and commentary can be found at *TIME*, BBC World Service, *USA Today*, *HuffPost*, *Christian Century*, *On Being*, *Sojourners*, and *Faith and Leadership*. She is a Ph.D. student in religious studies at Indiana University, where she and her Presbyterian minister-spouse live with their three kids in Hoosier country.

I look up to the mountains;
does my strength come from
    mountains?
No, my strength comes from God,
who made heaven, and earth,
    and mountains.

—PSALM 121:1–2 MSG

THE HOLY IS HERE,
PRESENT WITH ME:
A GUIDED MEDITATION

. . .

by Rev. Emily Swan

*I*N MY CONGREGATION WE SHIFT EASILY BETWEEN pronouns for God, and you'll notice I do so in this meditation. If you find that distracting, employ whatever pronouns you find helpful. I wanted to use feminine pronouns for the Habakkuk meditation because I think it's a powerful image in our time and cultural setting.

Find someplace comfortable. Relax. Breathe deeply, in through your nose and out through your mouth. If it's helpful, you can use a mantra to calm your thoughts as you breathe.

[Breathe in.] The holy is here,
[Breathe out.] present with me.

Close your eyes. Picture yourself sitting in a place, real or imaginary, that gives you joy. Notice your surroundings. What are you sitting on? Do you smell anything? What do you hear? See? Feel? Taste?

Meditate on Habakkuk 2:20 for a couple of minutes.

You can start by using the verse as a mantra in rhythm with your breaths.

> *[Breathe in.] The Lord is in her holy temple;*
> *[Breathe out.] let all the earth be silent*
>   *before her.*

After you've focused on the verse for a while, let your mind's eye view the earth as a temple of God. Don't rush—give yourself time to look at your surroundings. Imagine others around the world also being silent in the presence of this God. Feel their camaraderie—that they, also, are following the Spirit of Love. Linger and observe what happens, if anything. Give God space to speak, if they want.

Now, imagine this God (as Jesus, or however you picture God) comes and sits or hovers nearby. Where are they in relation to you? How does it feel? In this space, pray whatever comes to mind. Ask questions. Make petitions. Sit in awe. Get angry. If you want, make space for God to converse with you, if they want to do so.

Imagine there's a low table in front of you, filled with candles. What does it look like? Pick up a box of matches and light a candle for each burden weighing your mind. Ask God to turn their face towards the lights. God may have something to say about one or two of the candles, or perhaps you sit in silence, experiencing the attention of the Presence.

Feel God's love and enjoyment of you. (If you can't feel this, perhaps ask them why.) Invite the Spirit to continue filling and empowering you as you move ahead in your day or week.

Close with this Prayer for the Church:

A PRAYER FOR THE CHURCH

Spirit of Jesus—
Come with fire that refines,
Water that refreshes,
Wind that topples,
Breath that fills.

Kindle a global revival of empathy, justice, and
*   active peacemaking.*
Birth a witness of Love that is bigger and better
*   than we inherited.*
Liberate us from privilege and oppression.
Unshackle the gospel from nationalism, colonial-
*   ism, white supremacy, and every other lens*
*   that shrouds the Good News.*
Give us an abundance of grace for others and
*   ourselves.*
Grant us compassion for those who suffer.
Free us from the influence of money, power, and
*   acclaim.*

*Restore our reputation for caring for the poor,
        loving our neighbors, being ambassadors of
        peace and stewards of the earth.*
*Unlock the immense resources hoarded in the
        Western Church and release them for your
        name's sake.*
*Encourage us, so we do not grow cynical,
        isolated, and burnt-out.*
Fan our hopes, our joys, and our connections.
Allow us rest when we need rest.
Enable us to see you in each person we encounter.
Show us mercy, in our humanity.

Let us love more fully than we thought possible.
*Let us not be quick on the draw, ready to retali-
        ate, escalate, assassinate.*
*Let our collective fervor for justice eclipse institu-
        tional concerns.*
*Let us trust and follow the wisdom of those who
        have been marginalized.*
*Let us persevere in creating safe places of worship
        to eat bread and drink wine together.*

Let us stand for *Love and* with *Love, following
        the way of your Son as best we're able.*
Let us not fear an experiential spirituality.
Let us listen to the wondrous bodies you gave us.

Let us hear your voice and tangibly feel you
with us.
Let us discern your guidance.
Let us abide in and with you.

Show us what you're doing, so we can work
together. Move where you will, when you
will, in whatever way you will. Come,
Holy Spirit, and restore your Church.

Amen.

REV. EMILY SWAN is the co-founder and co-pastor (along with Ken Wilson) of Blue Ocean Church Ann Arbor. She received her B.A. in history from Butler University, and has worked toward her master's degree at Fuller Theological Seminary. Additionally, she spent three years studying Mandarin and Amdo Tibetan languages at Qinghai Minzu Dazue Nationalities University in Xining, China. Emily is co-author (along with Wilson) of *Solus Jesus: A Theology of Resistance,* winner of the 2020 Eric Hoffer Book Award in the spirituality category. Emily is married to Rachel Murr. They live in Ypsilanti with their cat, Lilo, and enjoy gardening and playing tennis.

Go where your best prayers take you.

—FREDERICK BUECHNER

FINDING REST

...

by Marlena Graves

*I*T IS THE LONGEST, DARKEST NIGHT OF THE YEAR. Almost Christmas. Here I am hunched over, nearly collapsing under the weight of the world.

It is too heavy.

I am burdened for the children all over the world who in this very moment are being sexually, physically, and verbally abused. Right now, it is happening as I sit attempting to pray.

This same thought plagues me regularly. The problem of evil.

I think of the hungry. Those sleeping on the streets while I have the luxury of a heated home. About the teenagers I know personally who will get little to nothing for Christmas. Last year they begged us to hold office hours during Thanksgiving and Christmas vacation so they could have something to do, something to break up the misery and monotony, the loneliness and despair, of a long school break. Part of our work entails mentoring and educating inner-city youth in employment readiness, educational empowerment, and community service in an after-school program. Our office is a safe and warm place—without stress. Growing up, I too hated Thanksgiving and Christmas. There was little food and few, if any, gifts. If I did get a gift, it was a regift that was a free gift, from my mom, like a woman's purse. Nothing for a child. There were no bright holidays or expectations that I imagined resided in other households.

For many, including some of the teenagers in our program, winter break means no school breakfast, lunch, or after-school program snacks. Kids are cold because they have no heat in their homes. They can see their breath crystalize inside of the house. I know this. I experienced seeing my own breath inside of my home and having to sleep with my jacket on under a pile of covers. Sometimes we used the oven to warm ourselves. School in session meant warmth and food.

I think of the elderly. Lonely and tucked away in nursing homes, or their own homes, longing so desperately for the physical presence of another. Their companion? A flickering TV. Our society closets the elderly and elevates the young. To our detriment, we do not avail ourselves of the wisdom and beauty of the elderly. We quarantine ourselves from aging, sickness, and death. And yet we are dying. The suicide rate climbs sky-high.

These are things I think about all at once.

One of my own family members is worried about cancer. A continent is burning. Our "Christian nation" is putting kids in cages, separating families, herding people into dangerous ghettos in Juarez—being hell to those trying to escape it.

This is why I fold under this weight.

Jesus! Jesus, how did you do it? How did you manage with war, rumors of wars, sickness, and pain all about you, with oppression, rejection by family, friends, and foes alike? How did you manage with the knowledge you would suffer in such an excruciating way?

Me? I cannot save the world. I can barely get myself together. My sins are many. I have little power, little sway. Little money. What can be done? What can any of us really do?

In all this, you bid me come. "Come to me, all you who are weary and burdened, and I will give you rest. Take my yoke upon you and learn from me, for I am gentle and humble in heart, and you will find rest for your souls" (Matthew 11:28–29).

Jesus, I come to you.

Could your yoke, or teaching, have something to do with me offering my five loaves and two fish, like the little boy? Offering the little I have and in some way being part of the answer to many prayers? Is it in trusting you, Triune God, to multiply my offering and the offerings of others wherever they find themselves?

Oh, I see.

You *do* see.

You don't expect me to save the world. I literally cannot. That is your work. But you do expect me to do and love to the best of my ability in any given moment, right? To cry for them like you did Lazarus. And maybe if I do that, see them and cry for them and do my part with what I have, it'll be enough. It is all you ask: no more, no less. And all that I can do. I can relax knowing you and others pick up where I leave off.

Take care of those I mentioned this night. Send your angels for them. Send people. Give concrete help. Multiply our offerings. I know I can trust you. You are good. You love them and are making all things new even now. With all my heart I believe this.

Amen.

MARLENA GRAVES is the author of the *The Way Up Is Down: Becoming Yourself by Forgetting Yourself* and *A Beautiful Disaster: Finding Hope in the Midst of Brokenness*. Her articles can be found in a variety of venues. She is passionate about, and works for, the human rights of immigrants, migrant farm workers, and those in poverty. She is pursuing her Ph.D. in American Culture Studies at Bowling Green State University and lives with her husband and three daughters in the Toledo, Ohio, area.

Let gratitude be the pillow upon which you kneel to say your nightly prayer. And let faith be the bridge you build to overcome evil and welcome good.

—MAYA ANGELOU

RECONCILIATION SOUP

...

by Osheta Moore

I NEVER KNEW YOU COULD MAKE CHICKEN NOODLE soup from scratch. Like sliced bread and chewy chocolate cookies, I thought there were secrets to making comfort foods that only grocery stores knew. In my family, if the flu struck, Mama would bring a can of Campbell's. This was the "recipe" of comfort foods of my past.

One day, while reading a cookbook, I found a recipe for chicken noodle soup and realized that women just like me have been creating this alchemy of stock and vegetables, starch and spice, simmered and served for hundreds of years before me. Making soup didn't feel as unattainable as I once thought. The ingredients were already in my kitchen and my hands were capable, so I made it my mission to master the chicken noodle soup—my ultimate comfort food.

These days, with racism dividing us, I've noticed I'm making chicken noodle soup more often. It feels like the infection of racism is nowhere near rooted out, no matter how much we'd like to think so.

As a Black woman, I still see it. Every day. In crafty, insidious ways. Like when a white co-worker confuses me for the only other person of color in the office—even though we look nothing alike—or when a well-meaning elderly lady asks me, a darker brown-skinned woman, if I'm the nanny to my three light-skinned biracial kids. Racism infects everyday social interactions for the African American person. Most of the time, it's as unnoticeable as the cold virus that sneaks around our system until we can't take it anymore and *cough, cough, cough,* we're unable to move out of bed. Racism slips quietly into our thinking, forming negative stories, reinforcing undeserved pride, and shaping accusations. Until suddenly, *pop, pop, pop,* Black bodies lie dying in the street and we're unable to move forward.

I try to give my white brothers and sisters the benefit of the doubt. I try so hard to not let my children see my anxiety and mistrust, but I don't want to hold my boy's bullet-riddled body and wonder "What could I have told him to do to make the white people comfortable around him to prevent this?" I'm fighting my own overgeneralizations and my impulse to demonize decent people trapped in an unjust system, but it's hard. I want to listen to their stories, but I'm infected, too.

So, I made my soup.

I once heard of a monk who prayed while he washed dishes. I like that, so I pray while making soup and call it my "reconciliation soup."

PREPARE CHICKEN: Just like I take care to avoid the dangers of raw chicken, Jesus helps me handle reconciliation with care. It's full of possibilities to hurt. Like the salmonella that coats this very chicken, scary and dangerous and off-putting. I want to avoid handling it, but I can't. It's as vital to this soup as racial justice is to your Kingdom. It's essential to our formation into people who want to look like you. I respect the gritty nature of holding flesh in my hands, so I'm careful, and afterward I wash everything thoroughly. Help me know how to respond to the raw words of fear and pride with care. Then let me thoroughly wash every interaction in grace.

DICE ONIONS: Jesus, help me embrace the tears. Tears are not my enemy—they are indications of prayers needing to be prayed, maybe even with childlike faith. Help me pray the deep prayers of unity as I dice and measure.

SLICE CARROTS: Some say eating carrots gives you good eyesight. If so, Jesus, I want to see people as Beloveds. White and Black. Police officer and politician. Story breakers and stay-at-home moms. They are all valuable to you, so they will be valuable to me.

CHOP CELERY: I don't understand celery, Lord. Its punchy, sharp, bitter taste seems too much for this soup. Too bold. Overpowering. But simmered with the other ingredients, it helps create a healing broth. Lord, my anger feels like celery. I don't understand it; it's too much. I ask you to take it, turn it into something useful.

Let it simmer mixed in with your love and wisdom until it creates something life-giving. Every recipe for chicken noodle soup calls for the celery, so I'll use it. Every act of reconciliation calls for a safe space for sharp words and hard truths, so I'll use them and trust they will transform relationships like the celery transforms the soup.

TOSS IN ANY LEFTOVER FROZEN VEGGIES: Jesus, thank you that in the Father's economy, nothing is wasted! Not our fears, not our tears, not our questions, and most definitely, not our prayers. Especially when we pray for your shalom. Lord, take our prayers that sometimes feel inadequate and use them to make a banquet table of hope before us.

ADD NOODLES: Lord, let us remember that we are intertwined. Let us not shy away from bumping into each other in the broth of reconciliation. Let us wrap around each other and soften our wills to yours.

BRING TO BOIL: Because the ingredients are only changed under pressure when the heat seems unbearable and the broth permeates the noodles' hardness, Jesus, refine us in your fire. Let us submit to the heat of your call to unity because it brings the warmth of wholeness, the warmth of the Kingdom of God here on earth as it is in heaven.

Simmer until the aroma of peace fills your kitchen and serve.

OSHETA MOORE is a pastor who is convinced God has a sense of humor. Osheta is the author of *Shalom Sistas: Living Wholeheartedly in a Brokenhearted World*, on everyday peacemaking. She is also an ESFJ mama who loves parties, people, and popcorn with red wine. Osheta loves Jesus a lot and cusses . . . a little. She's an optimistic cookbook reader, a hopeless romantic, and a goofball with a little bit of sass.

*Prayer is nothing else
than being on terms
of friendship with God.*

—TERESA OF AVILA

A PRAYER TO
BREATHE

. . .

by Sarah Bessey

*B*REATH PRAYER IS AN ANCIENT FORM OF PRAYER easily adaptable for anyone. Simply choose one or two lines to meditate on, and inhale and then exhale through them. One common form of breath prayer is known as the Jesus Prayer:

(From Matthew 11:28–30)
Inhale: *Humble and gentle One,*
Exhale: *you are rest for my soul.*
(From John 15)
Inhale: *True Vine and Gardener,*
Exhale: *I abide in You.*
(From Romans 8:38–39)
Inhale: *Nothing can separate me,*
Exhale: *from the love of God.*
(From Psalm 46:10)
Inhale: *Be still*
Exhale: *and know you are God.*
(From Matt. 6:10)

Inhale: *On earth*
Exhale: *as it is in heaven.*
(From 2 Cor. 12:9)
Inhale: *Your grace*
Exhale: *is enough for me.*
(From 1 John)
Inhale: *There is no fear*
Exhale: *in your Love.*
(From Psalm 23)
Inhale: *I will not be afraid*
Exhale: *for You are with me.*
(From Psalm 46:1)
Inhale: *You are our refuge*
Exhale: *and our strength.*
(From Psalm 74:16)
Inhale: *Both day and night*
Exhale: *belong to You.*
(From Psalm 91:1)
Inhale: *I find rest*
Exhale: *in Your shelter.*
(From Psalm 103: 4–5)
Inhale: *You surround me with love*
Exhale: *and tender mercies.*
Inhale: *You fill my life*
Exhale: *with good things.*
(From Philippians 4:7)
Inhale: *Peace of Christ,*
Exhale: *guard my heart and mind.*

Start with ten good breaths in and out, with
the words that are most meaningful or
steadying to your soul.

Disorientation

I will have nothing to do with a God who cares
only occasionally. I need a God who is with us
always, everywhere, in the deepest depths as
well as the highest heights. It is when things go
wrong, when the good things do not happen,
when our prayers seem to have been lost,
that God is most present. We do not need the
sheltering wings when things go smoothly.
We are closest to God in the darkness,
stumbling along blindly.

—MADELEINE L'ENGLE

THE FOOLISHNESS OF
A KINGDOM

...

by Alia Joy

I READ SOMEWHERE THAT BLACK HOLES ARE ONE OF the heaviest objects in the universe, their gravity so dense that even light gets trapped. I don't claim to understand the science of cosmic things but I know about the weight of darkness, of empty space, of its pull and gravity. I'm a woman with a medical file that stretches like the belly of an accordion, filled with tests, procedures, and diagnoses—but I'm incurable. At best, I can only hope to be managed with an antipsychotic, an antidepressant, and a medley of other meds and healthy life practices.

Still, I know the meteoric rise of mania when my limbs are lusty and incandescent. I see patterns connecting my words like constellations. I am celestial. I chatter to God incessantly. And on nights when my pillow can't hold my head, too full of moonlight ruminations, I bake a cobbler, read beautiful writing with a sturdy wool throw on my lap and my dog curled at my side. I'll thank God for Nina Simone's music as "Feeling Good" pounds in my earbuds. Eventually, I'll tangle my legs in the sheets, searching for silence and sleep.

But at the height of my bipolar disorder, my prayers become starbursts: they explode from me, illuminating my universe. My mind is too bright for sleep, so I rise and stand barefoot in my kitchen, letting my heart fill with adoration:

Thank you, Jesus, for nontoxic cleaners that smell like honeysuckle (especially when insomnia keeps me up for days and I scrub the cracks in the kitchen floor with a toothbrush at three in the morning) and for the way Finn wags himself sideways like a furry little drunk when I come home, and peach cobbler, and the cool spot my wandering legs find in my sheets, and Brian Doyle's writing, although we lost him too soon so I won't say thanks for that because death is a catastrophe, but still, thanks for the words he left behind, they've helped. And hoping words are the best kind. And knitting, although I don't knit but still I'm thankful to live in a world where it's an option because I've wanted to learn. And yarn animals! I can think of three— alpaca, sheep, and what was the other one? I forget. Goat? Can you shear a goat? Goat yarn? I don't know but thank you, God, for having the fore-thought of a shepherd and for your creation of woolly animals. You get what it feels like to be naked and exposed, and you weave together all that covers and binds us. Your kingdom is limitless because yarn can also be made from bamboo, silk, hemp, cotton . . . and then there are factories making synthetic yarn out of chemicals and science and isn't that a miracle too? That elements from the periodic table are mixed in a vat and out comes a sweater? I'm sure there's more to it than that but just that we come up with this stuff, that people actually make use of math with exponentials and X's and Y's, all *Good Will Hunting* style and science beyond Bunsen burners and baking soda volcanoes. Unless the science-y math part harms the environment, or unfairly treats workers who're making yarn or sweaters, or alpacas. Then never mind about that part. And since I've no use for fancy math or science, I once again thank you for the language of hope I dabble in. Amen.

In the morning, my prayers become actions. I drive myself 26.6 miles to the craft store. My arms stretch like angel wings as I run my fingers across the bins of yarn with dye lot numbers, where blue is peacock, canard, and kingfisher. I gather a sea of skeins in Aegean and lapis against my breast, like a mother would her child, and carry the lot to the register.

"What are you knitting?" the clerk asks me as she rings up my mountain of yarn.

"A sweater, I think. I haven't gotten that far. I'm going to teach myself." I reply with the bravado of a woman who will drive the 26.6 miles home and immediately download a pattern as complicated as the swirling cosmos, certain that YouTube tutorials and days of dropping stitches and picking them back up with obsessive devotion will create something to withstand the cold.

But the mania won't last long enough to knit a blue sweater.

Back at home, it doesn't take long before needles stick out of the pile of yarn like flagpoles on a hill waiting for me to run up the white flag, surrendering my scattered prayers of thanks.

Where once I was celestial in my mania, floating, weightless, I reenter the atmosphere on a collision course. I am no stranger to the shattering devastation of this heavenly body returning to earth, crammed back into flesh that scars, imprisoned by a mind tightfisted around sorrow. I am embodied in brokenness, hellish in my depression. I know the body that cannot rise against the gravity of despair, let alone hands able to knit one, purl two. My vacant tongue lashes at the corners of my mouth as if ridding it of cobwebs. If lips could atrophy from disuse, mine would wither. The atmosphere feels too thick and suffocating for sound to reach the heavens. Only muffled cries and grunts of pain escape my mouth.

When my soul circles this black hole, a gratefulness for cobbler and cool sheets sounds ludicrous. Am I a weak, foolish woman who does little more than pay attention to silly things? But when I think of a God who "chose the foolish things of the world to shame the wise, the weak things of the world to shame the strong," maybe a world with kingfisher-blue alpaca yarn is more than enough to remember Jesus's loving tenderness. God's mercy tethers me to hope in the foolishness of a kingdom where childlike wonder, the ramblings of my manic mind, and my depressed groanings are liturgy. Is this what it means to pray without ceasing? A mind attentive to God's grace. A God near enough to hear my prayers.

I swish my legs across my sheets in search of the cool spot and I remember *Yours is the kingdom and the power and the glory*. And this prayer is enough for a weak, foolish woman like me. *Amen.*

ALIA JOY is a ragamuffin storyteller who has become a trusted voice in conversations around mental and physical illness, abuse, race, embodiment, poverty, and staying fluent in the language of hope. She is the author of *Glorious Weakness: Discovering God in All We Lack*, a deeply personal exploration of what it means to be poor in spirit. Sushi is her love language, and she balances her world-weary idealism with humor and awkward pauses. She lives in central Oregon with her husband, her tiny Asian mother, her three kids, a dog, a bunny, and a bunch of chickens.

If your heart is broken, you'll find God right there;
if you're kicked in the gut, he'll help you catch your breath.

—PSALM 34:18 MSG

PRAYER OF A WEARY
BLACK WOMAN

. . .

by Chanequa Walker-Barnes, Ph.D.

DEAR GOD,

Please help me to hate White people. Or at least to want to hate them. At least, I want to stop caring about them, individually and collectively. I want to stop caring about their misguided, racist souls, to stop believing that they can be better, that they can stop being racist.

I am not talking about the White antiracist allies who have taken up this struggle against racism with their whole lives—the ones who stand vigil for weeks outside jails where Black women are killed; who show up in Charlottesville and Ferguson and Baltimore and Pasadena to take a public stand against racism and police brutality; who are so committed to fighting White supremacy that their own lives bear the wounds of its scars.

No, those aren't the people I want to hate. I'm not even talking about the ardent racists, either, the strident segregationists who mow down nonviolent antiracist protesters, who open fire on Black churchgoers, or who plot acts of racial terrorism hoping to start a race war. Those people are already in hell. There's no need to waste hatred on them. Perhaps, however, you could make sure that they don't take the rest of us with them, that their attempts at harming others are thwarted, and that they don't gain access to positions of power.

My prayer is that you would help me to hate the other White people—you know, the nice ones. The Fox News–loving, Trump-supporting voters who "don't see color" but who make thinly veiled racist comments about "those people." The people who are happy to have me over for dinner but alert the neighborhood watch anytime an unrecognized person of color passes their house. The people who welcome Black people in their churches and small groups but brand us as heretics if we suggest that Christianity is concerned with the poor and the oppressed. The people who politely tell us that we can leave when we call out the racial microaggressions we experience in their ministries.

But since I don't have many relationships with people like that, perhaps they are not a good use of hatred either. Lord, grant me, then, the permission and desire to hate the White people who claim the progressive label but who are really wolves in sheep's clothing. Those who've learned enough history, read enough books, spent enough time in other countries to make themselves seem knowledgeable even though that knowledge remains far removed from their hearts. Those whose unexamined White supremacy bubbles up at times I'm not expecting it, when I have my guard down and my heart open. Lord, if you can't make me hate them, at least spare me from their perennial gaslighting, whiteman-splaining, and White woman tears.

Lord, if it be your will, harden my heart. Stop me from striving to see the best in people. Stop me from being hopeful that White people can do and be better. Let me imagine them instead as white-hooded robes standing in front of burning crosses. Let me see them as hopelessly unrepentant, reprobate bigots who have blasphemed the Holy Spirit and who need to be handed over to the evil one. Let me be like Jonah, unwilling for my enemies to change, or like Lot, able to walk away from them and their sinfulness without trying to call them to repentance. Let me stop seeing them as members of the same body.

Free me from this burden of calling them to confession and repentance. Grant me a Get Out of Judgment Free card if I make White people the exception to your commandment to love our neighbors as we love ourselves.

But I will trust in you, my Lord. You have kept my love and my hope steadfast even when they have trampled on it. You have rescued me from the monster of racism when it sought to devour me. You have lifted up my head when it was low and healed my heart when it was wounded.

You have not given me up to slavery or to Jim Crow or to the systems of structural oppression, but you have called me to be an agent in your ministry of justice and reconciliation.

And you have not allowed me to languish alone, but you have lighted the path towards beloved community with the loving witness of the ancestors, elders, and sojourners who have come before me and who stand with me today.

Thus, in the spirits of Fannie and Ida and Pauli and Ella and Septima and Coretta, I pray and I press on, in love.

Amen.

DR. CHANEQUA WALKER-BARNES is a clinical psychologist, womanist theologian, and ecumenical minister whose work focuses upon healing the legacies of racial and gender oppression. The author of *I Bring the Voices of My People: A Womanist Vision for Racial Reconciliation* and *Too Heavy a Yoke: Black Women and the Burden of Strength*, she currently serves as Associate Professor of Practical Theology at Mercer University. She was ordained by an independent fellowship that holds incarnational theology, community engagement, social justice, and prophetic witness as its core values.

A PRAYER FOR
THE TIRED, ANGRY ONES

...

by Laura Jean Truman

God,

We're so tired.

We want to do justice, but the work feels endless, and the results look so small in our exhausted hands.

We want to love mercy, but our enemies are relentless, and it feels like foolishness to prioritize gentleness in this unbelievably cruel world.

We want to walk humbly, but self-promotion is seductive, and we are afraid that if we don't look after ourselves, no one else will.

We want to be kind, but our anger feels insatiable.

Jesus, in this never-ending wilderness, come to us and grant us grace.

Grant us the courage to keep showing up to impossible battles, trusting that it is our commitment to faithfulness, and not our obsession with results, that will bring in Your *shalom*.

Grant us the vulnerability to risk loving our difficult and complicated neighbor, rejecting the lie

that some people are made more in the image
of God than others.

Grant us the humility of a decentered but Beloved
self.

As we continue to take the single step that is in
front of us, Jesus, keep us from becoming what
we are called to transform. Protect us from
using the empire's violence—in our words, in
our theology, in our activism, and in our
politics—for Your kingdom of peace.

Keep our anger from becoming meanness.

Keep our sorrow from collapsing into self-pity.

Keep our hearts soft enough to keep breaking.

Keep our outrage turned towards justice, not cru-
elty.

Remind us that all of this, every bit of it, is for
love.

Keep us fiercely kind.

Amen.

LAURA JEAN TRUMAN is a writer and substitute bartender living
in Atlanta, Georgia. She's passionate about the intersections
of queer spirituality, mysticism, and the Gospel. She holds a
B.A. in philosophy from the University of New Hampshire
and an MDiv from Emory University: Candler School of
Theology. Follow her on Twitter and Instagram @Laura
JeanTruman and on her blog at laurajeantruman.com.

I yell out to my God, I yell with all
  my might,
I yell at the top of my lungs. He listens.
I found myself in trouble and went
  looking for my Lord;
My life was an open wound that
  wouldn't heal.
When friends said, "Everything will
  turn out all right,"
I didn't believe a word they said.
I remember God—and shake my head.
I bow my head—then wring my hands.

—PSALM 77:1–3 MSG

A PRAYER FOR WHEN YOU DON'T EVEN KNOW WHAT YOU WANT

...

by Sarah Bessey

Settle down into the silence. Close your eyes.

Inhale.

Speak the name of God that rises to your lips:

Jesus, Mother, Abba, Yahweh, Father, God, Spirit, simply let it be what it is.

Exhale.

Imagine God calling you by your name.

And hear God say to you, as Jesus said to the blind man who called out to him,

What do you want me to do for you?

Inhale. Exhale.

And answer honestly.

I do not understand the mystery of grace—
only that it meets us where we are
and does not leave us where it found us.

—ANNE LAMOTT

A LITURGY FOR
DISABILITY

...

by Stephanie Tait

*T*HIS PRAYER IS DESIGNED TO LEAD A GROUP IN A *traditional call-and-response-style liturgy familiar to many mainline denominations, with the italicized lines indicating they are meant to be read in unison. Even if this sort of practice is unfamiliar to your particular faith tradition, consider leading a group together in this communal prayer. There is something profoundly powerful about acknowledging that we exist not only as individuals, but as pieces of our larger communities and of the collective body of Christ.*

Show us your glory.
Lord, you've heard these words offered count-
    less times, in songs of worship or the
    pleadings of prayer.
Show us your face, Lord. We want to see you.
    We want to witness your glory on display.
And yet we come with hearts of repentance,
    as we acknowledge the ways we have too
    often denied your glory displayed before
    us in disabled bodies.

Together we confess our sin. We lament the
sin of ableism.

Jesus, you who have victoriously conquered
death, remind us of the wounds you still
bear in your resurrection. Teach us like
you did Thomas, saying, "Put your finger
here. Look at my hands. Put your hand
into my side. No more disbelief. Believe!"*

We worship you, our wounded king.

God our creator, reveal the ways we have
discounted the beauty of your intention-
ally diverse design. Teach us like you did
Moses, saying, "Who has made man's
mouth? Who makes him mute, or deaf, or
seeing, or blind? Is it not I, the Lord?"†

Thank you for the beauty of your diverse
creation. We see your image more clearly
displayed through our differences.

Convict us, Lord, of the ways we have
harmed those who are disabled with our
belief, whether spoken or unspoken, that
they may be experiencing punishment for
sin. Teach us like you did your disciples,
saying, "Neither they nor their parents
have sinned. This happened so that God's

---

* John 20:27 CEB.

† Exodus 4:11 CEB.

mighty works might be displayed in them."*

Lord, liberate those who are disabled from our judgements and false assumptions, and release them from the added burden of doubt and shame.

Search our hearts and expose our pride. Dismantle our idols of self-reliance and the illusion of meritocracy. Show us the ways we ignore our privilege and claim credit for your heavenly mercies as personal accomplishment. Give us the wisdom of Solomon, saying, "The fastest runner doesn't always win the race, and the strongest warrior doesn't always win the battle. The wise sometimes go hungry, and the skillful are not necessarily wealthy. And those who are educated don't always lead successful lives. But time and chance happen to them all."†

We confess the sin of our pride and renounce the lie of meritocracy. Teach us to follow the example of Paul, by refusing to boast of anything except our own weakness, in

---

* John 9:3 CEB, edited for inclusive language.

† Ecclesiastes 9:11 NLT and NIV.

which your power is all the more fully displayed.*

God of love, show us the ways we have ex-
cluded disabled bodies from our tables,
from our pews, and from our pulpits. Reveal the ways we have belittled or discounted the giftings of disabled people.
Teach us how to make a place where they
are not only welcome to receive, but where
they are empowered to serve, teach, and
lead us as well. Remind us of the blueprint
scripture offers for a thriving and unified
body of believers, saying, "The parts of
the body that people think are the weakest
are the most necessary, which is why God
designed the body to give greater honor to
those parts, so that there won't be division
in the body."†

Show us how to wholly welcome disabled
bodies in our churches, homes, and communities. Teach us to better honor them
for their vital role in your Kingdom.

Lord, use us to bring justice for those who are
disabled. Whether in our church, in our

---

* 2 Corinthians 11:30 and 12:9.

† 1 Corinthians 12:22, 24–25, edited for clarity.

community, or throughout the world, we
pray that they would experience dignity,
acceptance, and belonging. We ask that
they be fully empowered to serve your
Kingdom, and find freedom from the bar-
riers of prejudice and discrimination.

Let the change begin with us. Rid us of the sin
of ableism, and lead us in the way of your
justice—on earth as it is in heaven.

Amen.

As an author, speaker, disability advocate, and trauma survi-
vor, STEPHANIE TAIT has harnessed her experience, writing her
intimate understanding of pain into messages that foster healing within the Kingdom of God. With radical candor and
transparency, her work aims to partner sound theology and
practice with the unashamed acceptance of struggle in the
present tense. Her book, *The View from Rock Bottom*, exam-
ines the influences of the prosperity gospel in the modern
church and urges us to a deeper and more robust theology of
suffering.

Love your enemies
and pray for those
who persecute you.

—JESUS, Matthew 5:44

A PRAYER FOR
AMERICA

. . .

by Lisa Sharon Harper

Holy Holy Holy God,
We call her America for short.
When we speak her whole name, it fills the earth
  and edges you out.
Her name is United.
It is Stately.
It is Empire.
It is White.

With awe and honor and brutality and genocide
  and exploitation
Of Native American and African and Mexican and
  Chinese
Mothers, fathers, sisters, brothers
Families are exploited here
Families are broken here
Children scream for their broken or removed
  fathers
in their mother tongues here

Bàbá!
Padre!
父...
Papa!!!!

Hoe cracks earth and breaks back
Thin lips part in the form of a smile
They do not see—they choose not to see—
Now we choose not to see—
The tobacco and rice and cotton and sugar
And oil
And gas
Are plucked and pulled and drilled and fracked
    from the earth
Comfort drapes over our bodies and bank
    accounts
Like white crinoline petticoats
And over our fingers like opera gloves.
We, America, cover ourselves in whitewashed
    crinoline
That looks white to the world,
But underneath, our skirts are packed with the
    blood and bones of the dead.
And we sway in the wind. We like the look of our
    crinoline in the wind.
Only tiny pools of blood at our feet give our secret
    away.

We sway . . . and we smile
At least we are comfortable.
At least our red KitchenAid mixers sit neatly on
　　our counters.
And at least our children are able to attend
　　Montessori and the university and graduate
　　and own two cars and make two babies and
　　commute to work and at least their children
　　will know what it is like to grow up with a
　　nanny.
And at least our daughters' weddings don't break
　　the bank. Our bank is big.
And at least we have our 401(k)s—even after the
　　crisis.
And at least we can call ourselves the greatest
　　nation on earth—America.

But under our feet workers' cries push through
　　earth.
Muffled screams six feet under topsoil and
　　Miracle-Gro
They wail: "Poverty should not be my day's
　　wage!"
And under our feet Black mothers sob: "Cancer
　　took my baby! It crept into our home from
　　rancid water—contaminated, ignored and
　　dismissed. My little girl was dismissed."

And under our feet Latinx families are torn
    asunder.
Children ripped from mothers' arms.
They sit in cages
On concrete
Thousands cry: "Donde esta, Mami? "Quiero a mi
    papi!"

And on the other side of the veneer of perfect
    whiteness.
The softer set struggle to survive the domination
    of men disenfranchised by their own votes
    against "the other."
What they didn't know was the other is them.
As long as they give poor and working white men,
    give the nod to societies built on human hierar-
    chies of belonging
As long as they shake hands with the devil, they
    will chase whiteness and they will never find it.
    For it is only an illusion.
But in the meantime, they will blame foreigners
    and gays and women's libbers and The Blacks
    and The Mexicans
And they will blame China and the Middle
    East and liberals for threatening their
    whiteness
And they will hold their boots steady on the necks

of Black men pulled over for driving while
Black
And they will vote to restrict voting and job access
and ordination and reproductive services
And they will jury-rig elections and trials and
hearings and the law—simply because they
can—because that's what it means to be a
white man. You can.
And their women will join them, because they
shook hands with the devil's wife.
They know they are not white men, but at least
they can be white. At least they can have some
power.
The formative years of America taught them how
things work. They, too, were owned. They,
too, were ripped from their children. They, too,
were raped by their husbands.
They know beyond knowing: Without whiteness,
white women are nothing in America. And
being nothing is not an option.
So, arms attached to bodies shrunken to the point
of barely being seen lift size zero hands and
clasp in compact with Mrs. Satan.
And they all sing: "How Great Thou Art!"

This is how it has been.
This compact is leading our nation and the church
to its end.

Oh, God! Intervene!

Save us!

Strike Saul from his horse again!

Get in his face and ask him: "Why are you waging
    war against my image in your land?"

Rip scales from eyes before it is too late, Oh, God!

Help them to see.

Help us to see.

Help us all to see.

Amen.

LISA SHARON HARPER is the founder and president of Freedom Road, a groundbreaking consulting group that crafts experiences that bring common understanding and common commitments that lead to common action toward a more just world. Lisa is a public theologian whose writing, speaking, activism, and training has sparked and fed the fires of reformation in the church from Ferguson and Charlottesville to South Africa, Brazil, Australia, and Ireland. Lisa's book, *The Very Good Gospel*, was named 2016 Book of the Year and the *HuffPost* identified Lisa as one of 50 Women Religious Leaders to Celebrate on International Women's Day.

Going through the motions doesn't
  please you,
a flawless performance is nothing
  to you.
I learned God-worship
when my pride was shattered.
Heart-shattered lives ready for love
don't for a moment escape
  God's notice.

—PSALM 51:16–17 MSG

A LETTER TO MY FUTURE SELF IN THE FACE OF CHRONIC CRISIS

...

by Alicia T. Crosby

Dearest Future Me,

I thought I'd take a few moments and pen a letter to you.

Consider this a break in case of emergency. Well, maybe not emergency, but as you need, because your body is changing in some new and uncomfortable ways so what was once emergent is now recurrent.

I know myself well enough to give you tools to bust out in case chronic crisis waves knock you flat on your ass, which is why I'm writing this now.

Some days you will feel like shhh . . . Sugar Honey Iced Trash,

Pain mounting,
Feet swelling,
Cramp cramping,
Nerve exposed,
Garbage.
Your anxiety will rise up,
depression may set in,

And you'll feel every ounce of the fragility that lies in the concepts of health or wellness

'Cause, honey, those things are fleeting as hell.

When those days come, know you have options.

Some days it will take a bit of effort to get out of bed to do things you need to do for your sake or for those you love.

Other days will only afford you the energy to shuffle between your bed, bathroom, and couch when your state of being leads you to give thanks for Netflix and the kind human who delivers groceries and prepared food to your door because leaving the house was not an option.

But know that whether you stay home or choose to brave the world, whether you rally and go outside or submit to the comfort you find in your blankets and your bed, what you do is valid, your body is a gift, and you should treat her kindly.

She has gotten you to where you are, so find ways to be responsive to her and give her care.

Pray over her and press pause, if only for a moment, to hear her and her needs. Celebrate her, nourish her, comfort her, listen to her, grieve with her, be gracious with her, and treat her with tenderness.

Show her, show me, show us, show your present self that you too are worthy of the love that you so freely give to the world by first extending it to yourself.

ALICIA T. CROSBY (she/hers) is a justice educator, activist, and (sometimes reluctant) minister whose work addresses the spiritual, systemic, and interpersonal harm people experience. Through her writing, speaking, and space curation, Alicia helps individuals, communities, and institutions explore and unpack topics related to identity, inclusivity, and intersectional equity. You can follow her work via aliciatcrosby.com or on Facebook, Twitter, and Instagram via @aliciatcrosby.

Love and Truth meet in the street,

Right Living and Whole Living
    embrace and kiss!

Truth sprouts green from the ground,

Right Living pours down from the skies!

Oh yes! God gives Goodness and
    Beauty;

Our land responds with Bounty
    and Blessing.

Right Living strides out before him

And clears a path for his passage.

—PSALM 85:10–13 MSG

EXAMEN YOUR POLITICS

...

by Nish Weiseth

SPIRITUAL FORMATION IS THE PROCESS BY WHICH we are shaped by the power of the Holy Spirit into the image of Jesus for the sake of others. But none of the discipleship of my youth ever mentioned that we are made into the image of Jesus for the sake of others. Not for us, but for our neighbors, for our communities, for the sake of doing the work of Jesus here on *this* earth, in *this* time, to see the Kingdom of God break through the world just a little bit more tomorrow than it did today.

We are made more into the image of Jesus so that others might flourish, so that the last would be first, so that the poor in spirit, those who mourn, the meek, those who hunger and thirst for righteousness, the merciful, the pure in heart, the peacemakers, and the persecuted would be blessed.

We are called to be made more into the image of Jesus for *their* sake, so that they may be blessed. It is a formation that has others in the centre. When we are formed into the image of Jesus for the sake of others, only then will we have a politics that is formed by our faith, rather than the other way around.

Politics is the single largest systemic tool we have at our disposal with which we can love our neighbor. Simply put, politics for the Christian should be institutional neighborliness.

STARTED BY SAINT IGNATIUS of Loyola, the Prayer of Examen is an ancient practice and opportunity to reflect on our lives, observe the movement and presence of God, and more clearly discern His direction and guidance. It's a form of prayer that can rightly align our hearts with the heart of Christ, giving us the eyes to see what He sees, the love He has for others, and our role in illuminating the Kingdom of God.

What if we implemented this practice in our political engagement? After all, everything can be formative—for good and for bad. How are we being formed by our politics? More important, how are we letting God inform our political engagement?

Let's take the basic principles and outline of Ignatius's Prayer of Examen and place it within the context of our politics:

> Begin with a moment of quiet or silence. Close your eyes and make yourself as comfortable as

you're able. Take a deep breath. Allow yourself to awaken to the presence of God.

GRATITUDE

Thank God for today and the ability to make it through another day. Express your gratitude for any joys, victories, or encouragement you received. Thank Him for the people in your life. Tell Him thanks for the ability and opportunity to be politically engaged.

REQUEST

As you begin to review your political engagement, ask God for clarity about both your own self and about Him. Ask God to show you what you need to know.

REVIEW

Look back at your own involvement in politics—whether big (maybe you're running for office) or small (you read a piece of political news online). Ask yourself any or all of the following questions.

- What has troubled you about your own engagement?

- Where did you find joy in your political engagement?
- How did you love and serve others through your political actions today?
- Where did you feel challenged, or where did you feel opposition?
- When you participated in politics, what did you do well? What needs improvement?
- Be aware of your emotions—how do you think God sees you? How do you think He sees your politics?
- Where did you notice the presence and movement of God?
- How did you experience God's love?

YOUR RESPONSE TO GOD

After recalling your actions, reviewing your own engagement in politics, and reflecting on the movement of God, what is your response to God's revelations to you?

LOOKING FORWARD

What do you hope for in your own political engagement?

What do you desire from God?

How do you want to be formed tomorrow?

NISH WEISETH is a spiritual director and the founder of Formation Northwest, a contemplative living ministry for those seeking deeper intimacy with Christ. She lives in the mountains of Idaho with her husband, Erik, and two children, Rowan and Scout.

It is better in prayer
to have a heart without words
than words without heart.

—MAHATMA GANDHI

A PRAYER FOR THOSE
WHO CANNOT PRAY
WITH WORDS

. . .

PART
THREE

. . .

Reorientation

A PRAYER TO LEARN TO LOVE THE WORLD AGAIN

. . .

by Sarah Bessey

God of herons and heartbreak,
teach us to love the world again.
Teach us to love extravagantly
knowing it may
(it will) break our hearts
and teach us that it is worth it.

God of pandemics and suffering ones,
teach us to love the world again.

God of loneliness and longing,
of bushfires and wilderness,
of soup kitchens and border towns,
of snowfall and children,
teach us to love the world again.

Amen.

The wish to pray
is a prayer
in itself.

—GEORGES BERNANOS

THE LANTERN
AND THE
WILDFLOWER

. . .

by Kaitlin Curtice

If only I could give you
the gift of Adventure.
If only I could box her up
for you,
that big red bow on top,
glimmering.

But this cannot be.
Adventure is not
given or earned.
She is a breath that is prayed,
a force that is found,
found in the soul of everyone
and everything.

But maybe, just maybe,
if I cannot box her up for you,
I can at least point you
in her direction.
Maybe, at least,

I can tell you where I saw her last,
what I prayed when I was alone,
waiting in a forest under the pine trees,
waiting for her to appear.
Maybe that will be
your Beginning.

You see, I didn't learn for a long time.
For years, as soon as I began
searching,
I hid behind fear,
all the while,
Adventure waiting for me
with a lantern and wildflower.
All that time, I only wanted
pictures of her,
without knowing her presence,
her warmth,
her smell.

But when I met her,
I found myself.
When I prayed,
I found God.
If only I could teach you
not to be afraid.
If only I could tell you
that it's okay if you don't

have words left
to pray.

If only I could point you
towards that lantern
and that wildflower.
If only I could show you
the way to God.

But God cannot be given or earned.
No, *God is found*.
So, in that soul of yours,
there is the greatest opportunity.
You.
The world.
Breath and prayer embodied.
Everything sacred.
These things would never fit
into a box
with a big red bow on top,
glimmering.

KAITLIN CURTICE is a poet, author, and speaker. As an enrolled citizen of the Potawatomi Citizen Band and someone who has grown up in the Christian faith, Kaitlin writes on the intersection of Indigenous spirituality, faith in everyday life, and the church. Her new book, *Native* (available May 2020), is about identity, soul-searching, and being on the never-ending journey of finding ourselves and finding God. As both a citizen of the Potawatomi Nation and a Christian, Kaitlin Curtice offers a unique perspective on these topics. In this book, she shows how reconnecting with her identity both informs and challenges her faith.

If the only prayer you said
was thank you,
that would be enough.

—MEISTER ECKHART

FOR ALL THE
SO-CALLED LOST

...

by Rev. Emmy Kegler

> And what woman, if she had ten coins and lost
> one, wouldn't light a lamp, and sweep the house,
> and search diligently until she finds it?

—LUKE 15:8

Jesus, I am lost.

They told me to follow you
and I did—
to the edges, to the margins,
to the humble and grieving,
to the oppressed and slandered,
to where you always showed you were—
and when I called back to them
to show with joy what I had found,
to celebrate what had been restored,
they called me lost instead.

They call me wanderer,
they call me stubborn,

they call me black sheep.
It was supposed to be all green pastures
and still waters,
it was supposed to be all restored souls,
but all I could taste
were my unattended doubts,
and all that bubbled up
were troubled waters of unanswered questions,
and for asking them,
the shepherd said my soul was wrong.

They call me sinner,
they call me wasteful,
they call me prodigal,
and Jesus, I do not know how to tell them
the riches they say I stole
when I left the house of God
turned out to be pig slop.
I do not know how to tell them
how like you, I shared meals with sex workers,
and it was a feast of unending grace.

Jesus, today I heard how pennies
can't be made of copper anymore
because the amount of copper needed to make a
    penny
is more expensive than a penny is worth,
and Lord,

I feel it.
They ask me to be something smaller,
to be pressed down into something worth less,
to be crushed into something worthless.

Jesus, I have tried,
I have tried to be small enough,
I have tried to be shiny,
I have tried to be worthy,
but every time I press myself
with the imprint of someone else's expectations
it misses the mark
and I am left off-centre.

So here I am, Lord.
A quarter clinking around
in the bottom of the divine washing machine.
A nickel dropped under the car seat,
ground into a gritty floor.
A penny, slipping from a pocket,
rolled into a corner under the bed
where dust mites and bobby pins
are my only fellow believers.

Jesus, I need to see the broom in your hands.
I want to hear you turning over each empty
    pitcher
and shaking out every neatly folded sheet.

I need to see your belly pressed against the floor
and your dark eyes peering into my own darkness.
You know darkness, Lord.
It doesn't scare you.
You made it.
Long before your hands were bound in
    wrinkles and veins,
you crafted night and day, and you are afraid
    of neither.
But I am lost, and I am afraid.

Lord, they call me lost,
and if I am,
I want you to find me
the way you found the world:
nicked at the edges, dusty and rusty,
called unwanted and unworthy,
and still your hands reached out
to cradle every worthless coin
like each was a pearl of great price.

Jesus, in this congregation of the forgotten
    corner
I am finding I am not alone.
We are the church of the still lost
in the lost and found.
So when you come, bring a satchel
ready to collect what longs for home.

Jesus,
for every sheep and coin and child
called Lost,
may you pull us close and whisper,
"Found."

REV. EMMY KEGLER is a pastor, author, and speaker called to ministry at the margins of the church, especially among LGBTQ+ Christians. She serves as pastor of Grace Lutheran Church in Northeast Minneapolis, a small servant-hearted neighborhood congregation. She is a co-leader of the Queer Grace Community, a group of LGBTQ+ Christians in the Twin Cities. Her first book, *One Coin Found: How God's Love Stretches to the Margins,* details how her life as a queer Christian called to ordained ministry formed her relationship with Scripture. She lives in Saint Paul with her wife, Michelle, and their two dogs and cat.

Every morning,
You'll hear me at it again.
Every morning
I lay out the pieces of my life
on your altar
and watch for fire to descend.

—PSALM 5:3 MSG

A PRAYER FOR WHEN WE'VE LOST OUR WAY AGAIN

...

By Enuma Okoro

Merciful Lord,
sometimes it seems like we can't help but lose
    our way
again and again.
Our hearts long to follow you
but you know the way of the human heart.
You know how in our misguided longings we veer
    off our journeying to you
and begin to chart our own ways
by false stars and distorted visions.
Forgive us.
Forgive us for all the times we are tempted by the
    hints of light
instead of remaining steered by the assurance of
    Light.
Forgive us when we forget
that we are already claimed by you,
loved by you,
and purposed for you.
Forgive us when we allow ourselves

to shape and be shaped
by voices and words that do not bring life,
create life, nurture life, sustain life, or resurrect
    life.
Merciful God,
help us find our way again.
Turn us back towards the road
spotted with your other pilgrims, wayfarers, and
    repentant servants.
Remind us that your Way is the way of returning.
Guide us by your Spirit and by your Light.
Make us remember the Power of the Spirit
    within us.
Make us remember the gifts of our minds, our
    hearts, and our bodies that you have bestowed
    on us,
that we would use them to honor the directives
    and the invitations you lay upon us.
We know that our ways are not your ways.
And we thank you for this.
Help us trust your ways over our ways.
Remind us of your faithfulness as you forgive us
    our short memory.
In your immeasurable love, grace, mercy,
    and wisdom, do not abandon us
regardless of how often we lose our way.
Place your wounded hands upon our broken
    hearts and turn us towards you.

Lord of Light, Lord of the Life,
  Lord of Resurrection.
Amen.

ENUMA OKORO is a Nigerian-American writer and speaker whose work explores identity, culture, and the power of story. Raised in Côte d'Ivoire, England, North America, and Nigeria, she speaks globally at universities, organizations, corporate institutions, and conferences. Her TEDx talk focused on global perceptions of women, identity, and cultural diversity. In 2018 she was listed as one of 100 Most Inspiring Women in Nigeria. Currently at work on a novel, Okoro has published four books and her articles and essays have been featured in *The New York Times, The Atlantic Monthly, Aeon, Catapult,* CNN, the UK and US *Guardian, The Washington Post, Essence Magazine,* and other media outlets.

A CENTERING PRACTICE
FOR PRAYER

. . .

by Sarah Bessey

*B*ECOME AWARE OF YOUR BODY. SIT IN A WAY THAT is comfortable for you, a position that will allow you to take a deep breath. Close your eyes.

Bring to your mind and body a word or image that is meaningful to you, one that reminds you of God's faithfulness and presence and your own belovedness.

Breathe and hold that word or image for a few moments.

Then imagine a room or a place where you feel safe, your own sanctuary; it can be a real place or one that exists in your imagination. Imagine yourself in that sanctuary. Imagine the way the air smells and the way the light feels. Speak the name of God in that place.

Bring back the word or image you had earlier. Breathe and hold that word or image in your sanctuary space.

Enter into your time of prayer or meditation from within that sanctuary.

When you are finished, imagine yourself leaving that sanctuary. Transition slowly from prayer to rising.

He's God, our God, in charge of the
whole earth. And he remembers, remembers
his Covenant—for a thousand generations
he's been as good as his word.

—PSALM 105:7–8 MSG

ANCESTRAL WISDOM, PRESENT GUIDANCE

. . .

by Rozella Haydée White

*H*AVE YOU EVER STRUGGLED WITH KNOWING WHO you are? Have you ever wondered what steps to take next in life or in love? Have you ever felt like you were stumbling around in the dark, trying to figure out which way to go? Have you ever felt disconnected from yourself and from others?

There have been so many times in my life that I've experienced these things. Going through a divorce, battling depression, failing out of college, losing loved ones, watching plans I made disintegrate before my very eyes. All of these things left me reeling. I lost my sense of who I was (or who I thought I was) and felt like my ability to make any good decision was destroyed.

During these moments and others like it, I found myself in need of guidance. At one point I would have said that I needed someone to tell me what to do next. Just give me the right answer or show me the pathway and order my steps.

However, I soon realized that this was not what I truly needed. I didn't need guidance that told me just what decision to make or what steps to take.

I needed guidance that led me into the depths of my soul and my body. I needed guidance that was otherworldly, leading me on a journey that revealed the wisdom I was seeking. Much like the journey that George Bailey took in the movie *It's a Wonderful Life,* I needed guidance that showed me the truth of who I was, the reality of who I am, and the power of who I could be.

For much of my life, I tried the guidance of this world; guidance that came from intellect and from well-meaning folks who did not embody my lived reality. I found myself shifting and sifting through the advice and the information, struggling to make a connection with the guidance that I was given or pointed towards. None of it fit or seemed relevant to who I was or what I needed. I came to understand that the guidance I was seeking was one that tapped into the spirits of my ancestors: guidance that flowed from the women who came before me— Black and Brown women who were descendants of the Atlantic slave trade. Women whose bodies ended up in the Caribbean and on the southeastern shores of what came to be known as the United States of America. Women who faced every form of violence against their minds, hearts, bodies, and souls. Women who understood that life was more than what the eye could see. Women who refused to believe that their identities, experiences, and bodies were less than human, less than love, less than divine.

I needed and am continually in need of guidance that flows out of the embodied experiences of these women, guidance that taps into supernatural energy and reminds me of the power, wisdom, and love that are imprinted in the code of my DNA.

This world would have us believe that guidance and wisdom are rooted in the intellect and mind. However, our ancestral stories—if we take the time to listen and learn from them—show us that guidance and wisdom are rooted in our bodies: in our hearts and guts and limbs. This guidance is encoded in every nook and cranny of our physical beings and wants to make its way into our beliefs and behaviors.

Tapping into this guidance is a form of prayer. It requires stillness and deep listening. It requires care and attention to be paid to one's physical form. It asks the question "How is it with your soul?" and waits for the answer. It leads you to bear witness to your *whole* self—to your mind, body, heart, and soul.

Prayer is not about what you offer. It's about what you receive. Prayer invites us into Holy space and time that transcends *this* space and time. Prayer has the power to access deep wisdom and life-giving guidance that the Divine wants to share with us; wisdom and guidance that is informed by the long line of people who have come before us. Their experiences, their struggles, their joys, their faith all teach us something about ourselves. When we don't take the time to listen and reflect, we miss a part of our story.

I invite you to tap into the guidance that awaits us all.

Who are the women in your life who have come
before you?
What are their stories?
How did they embody their truth?
Where in your body do you feel this truth?
What is the Holy One revealing to you when
you listen to and learn from this truth?

May you listen and listen deeply to the guidance
and wisdom that is aching to be made known,
guidance and wisdom that you carry in your
body.
May this guidance and wisdom remind you of
who and whose you are.
May this guidance and wisdom reveal that you
are not alone.

ROZELLA HAYDÉE WHITE is a public theologian, spiritual life coach, leadership consultant, inspirational speaker, and writer, focused on nurturing life-giving and justice-seeking love in this world. She engages issues of faith, justice, self-awareness and love, mental illness, and the radical and transformative love of God as embodied in the person of Jesus. Known as the

#LoveBigCoach, she is the owner of RHW Consulting and believes that everyone is gifted and has the power to transform themselves, their communities, and the world when they take seriously their healing, fall in love with themselves and others, and align their beliefs and values with their behaviors. Rozella is the author of *Love Big: The Power of Revolutionary Relationships to Heal the World.*

I've thrown myself headlong into
  your arms—
I'm celebrating your rescue.
I'm singing at the top of my lungs,
I'm so full of answered prayers.

—PSALM 13:5–6 MSG

EMBODIED PRAYER

...

by Kelley Nikondeha

*P*RAYER FELT ETHEREAL AND OTHERWORLDLY IN MY youth. Whispered words vanished into air too thin to hold on to them. Did my prayers lack the necessary weight to weather this earth? And if so, how could my intangible intercessions transform the world?

Over the years, my prayer practices gained a physicality that grounded my prayers, ushering them into the earthly realm. For two years I used Spanish olive oil for daily meals, and each time I reached for the bottle I remembered to pray for friends living in Spain as they discerned their long-term vocation. I'd strike a match and light a vigil candle on the edge of my kitchen counter to pray for a friend travelling through Haiti. The flame flickered during the day, pulling me to pray again and again. Today I wear a silver key in solidarity with the people of Palestine, many of whom carry keys to homes they've yet to return to. Every morning when I put on the necklace, I pray for refugees the world over. These objects—olive oil, a candle, and a necklace—make prayer concrete.

I learned the more tangible the prayer, the more transformative potential it held for me. The act of incarnation gave weight to my petitions and my practice. The more I involved my five senses, the more full-bodied my prayer life became. The sound of church bells across Bethlehem calls me to pray, the aroma of incense hanging heavy against the arches in the Church of the Holy Sepulchre reminds me to add my prayers to those already ascended, and the bronzed patina sculpture of Mary and Elizabeth in the courtyard of the Church of the Visitation invites me to join these matriarchs in the work of tandem conversations and prayers. An incarnated prayer life can include places alongside senses, another lesson.

My most recent act of embodied prayer is the ancient practice of turning towards Jerusalem to pray. I discern the direction of the holy city, face her, and pray. In turning, I set my intention to intercede with my entire body. The redirection is more than physical; the posture of my heart follows. I lift my gaze from my own navel and towards a holy horizon that changes the trajectory of my prayers.

Historically Jews, Christians, and even Muslims prayed facing Jerusalem. The practice of the faithful centered on that hallowed place. I recognize that modern Jerusalem carries complexity, a holy and hotly contested city divided between faiths and factions. Maybe it's curious to make it central to my prayer life. And yet the current condition of the city is only a shell of the cityscape to come, according to the prophets.

Isaiah speaks of God doing a new thing—and fashioning a New Jerusalem with justice as its cornerstone is a centerpiece of his vision. In this New City swords will be melted into garden tools to feed the hungry and war colleges will be put out of business. Jubilee policies will recalibrate the economics of the city, creating equity for those who lived under the poverty line for too long. The eunuchs and foreigners, the widows and orphans, and all those surviving on the edges of society will experience durable hospitality. Women will survive childbirth, babies will reliably live beyond their second birthday, and people will see old age because there will be adequate health care. The prophet envisions the ever-open city gates welcoming people into the neighborliness of shalom and a shared worship space before God. Imagine such a place!

So I face Jerusalem, what it is and what it is to be, and pray from a point between the two cities. My prayers move from the individual sort centered on my comforts, my career growth, and my own safety towards intercession for my city full of resettled refugees and immigrants who, together with me, seek a collective wholeness where we are all safe, fed, and free. I pray with transformation in view for others who live at the mercy of unjust systems and without adequate resources. And then I pray for myself as part of those larger arcs towards justice.

Those prayers often lead me to join the campaign to dismantle empires instead of enjoying their benefits. Praying towards Jerusalem centers the deep desire for shalom for my neighbors and decenters my more provincial petitions. I plead for a home where all are safe, welcome, and embraced as kin. I turn towards the New City and am transformed.

These are the prayers that transform me and maybe the world. They are tangible as kingdom come.

KELLEY NIKONDEHA is a liberation theologian, writer, and community development practitioner. She lives between Burundi and the United States. She's authored *Adopted: The Sacrament of Belonging in a Fractured World* and *Defiant: What the Women of Exodus Teach Us About Freedom*.

INSTRUCTIONS FOR AN
EVENING OF YOUR LIFE

. . .

by Sarah Bessey

*F*IND A BIT OF WATER TO LOOK AT, IT DOESN'T HAVE
to be much. Maybe a pond, a river, a creek, a lake—if
you're really lucky, find the ocean. But go there alone at
sunset. I know it seems indulgent and impossible—that's
because it is. But every once in a while, the best way to
keep moving through your life is to do something that
seems impossibly kind for your own soul.

So go. Alone. Late in the day.

Leave behind the book. Leave behind your prayer
journal. Leave behind the notebooks and schedule plan-
ning. Leave behind the mobile phone—if you're in a
good spot, there won't be any reception anyways.

And here is your assignment: sit down and watch the
water.

That's exactly it.

Sit in silence at the edge of the water and learn to be
satisfied.

This is the tricky part when your life is full with good
and necessary and hard things, I know. Your mind will

jump around from thing to thing to thing. You'll feel guilty and then you'll feel indolent. You'll feel like time has slowed down.

You'll start to think that you need to make this time "count" for God and so you'll start to formally pray in the ways that you were taught to pray—stop that. Then you'll want to journal or read that about-God book you've been meaning to get to because you think you really need to grow spiritually and the only way to do that is to try harder. You'll get restless. You'll think of all the Things You Should Be Doing. You'll feel twitchy perhaps. Then you'll remember how when you were a kid you used to be able to just be in a place without compulsively needing to check text messages or chase around getting things done, and you'll think, *I didn't used to be so fragmented and urgent.*

Be silent and watch the water. Do one thing right now and do it with your whole self.

Prayer will come, it just might look a bit different than you expect. Rest will come to your mind, you have to wait for it in patience, this isn't the province of multi-taskers. The middle distance of your mind will rise up and envelop you in an exhalation just as the sun begins to move towards the horizon. You'll start to notice life as it is happening in that moment and this might begin to feel in your body like poetry is meant to sound.

A fish will fly up out of the water and return, leaving

only a ring of circles going farther and farther out to every shore. You'll see a bird and try to figure out what kind it is—a heron? Look at that elegant neck—swooping down low over the water heading for the reeds. You'll see dragonflies swooping and after a few times, you won't duck in a cringe anymore. You'll watch the clouds drift and the water move and the sun sink and your soul will begin to stretch out into the space left open. This is not only what you need—this is what you want, what you desire, and even those are sacred things at times. Before you know it, your hands will find a spot to rest and your breath will slow down.

Become acquainted with the silence in your own soul; you might be surprised by the sound of you. Sometimes you might rise up in gratitude and thanksgiving, other times the pain you're finally allowing yourself to feel might be overwhelming. Sometimes your soul feels like worship and sometimes this feels like encountering a stranger—do I know you? Then sometimes it might simply feel like a good friend you haven't seen in far too long and you'll think, *Why don't I do this more often?*

Let the sun set over the water. Be baptized in the gracious last light of the day, the satisfied light. Close your eyes and feel the light against your darkness, warming you.

When the sun has disappeared, the light remains. And

when the night sinks down in shades of indigo and navy blue, you'll be ready to be friends with the night and the silence, and hopefully with your own soul at last. The first star of the evening will appear at last like a benediction for the patient and faithful ones.

APPROACHING THE
MOUNTAIN IN PRAYER

. . .

by Barbara Brown Taylor

God Almighty.
God the Three in One.
Loving God.
Great Creator.

Dear God, I don't know how to begin my prayers
    anymore.
It's not that I want to go back to the way it was,
When I imagined you with your chin on your
    hand,
Inclining your ear to me like a patient confessor—
Or like a slightly more available father,
Who might be persuaded to give me what I wanted
In exchange for good behavior.

The longer I have known you, the more I have lost
    sight of you,
Which is not as bad as it sounds.
We are so close now that I can't imagine you with
    giant ears,

White eyebrows over golden eyes,
Massive hands that give or take by your inscruta-
    ble will.
There would have to be more distance between us
    for that.
We are so close now that you come to me as
    breath, pulse, wind, sap,
The steady humming current that weds all living
    things.

Imagine a mountain, I say to those who want to go
    there,
One so familiar you can see it with your eyes
    closed.
Green in summer, bare in winter, iridescent at sun-
    set,
It's always where it's supposed to be, right there
    on the horizon.
You have loved it from afar.

Now imagine deciding to climb that mountain,
Not once but over and over again—
First by the marked path, then by the deer trails,
Then by making your own way up.
One day you pray in the dry streambed.
One day you pray under the stone outcrop.
One day you pray facedown in the sweet birch
    leaves.

My point is, the better you know the mountain—
The more intimate you become—
The harder it is to see it whole, as something sepa-
     rate from yourself.
You're not looking at the mountain anymore.
You're not even on the mountain.
You're in the mountain's life, as its life pours into
     you.
This makes words hard to come by.

Oh Thou Who Art.
Thank you for green.
Wake me up to blue.
Receive the fine ash of my sadness.
Blow a seed my way.

Schooled in prayer, I hear what's missing:
Clarity of separation between creator and creation;
Attention to the needs of others;
Admission of my shortcomings;
A little more Christology, please.

These days I say so much less than that.
Thank God, dear God, you don't seem to mind.
We both like the words, because they mean I'm
     paying attention,
Though we both know the prayer is in the silence
     after.

Ragged breath becoming steady, then still,
Until I am all ears for you,
Here in the mountain of your presence
Where I can't see you anymore.

Oh Thou Who Art.
Breathe on me
And I shall be saved.

BARBARA BROWN TAYLOR is the *New York Times* bestselling author of *An Altar in the World*, *Learning to Walk in the Dark*, and *Holy Envy*. She has been an Avon lady, a cocktail waitress, a horseback riding instructor, and a hospital chaplain, but her favorite job was teaching World Religions at Piedmont College for twenty years before putting the chalk down in 2017. She now divides her time between writing, speaking, and caring for the land on which she lives. Barbara and her husband, Ed, tend a small farm in the foothills of the Appalachians.

Let your love, God,
shape my life.

—PSALM 119:41 MSG

A BENEDICTION

. . .

by Sarah Bessey

God of prayers for parking spots and prisons,
Of hospitals and holidays,
Of anger and angels,
Of traveling mercies and tired ones,
Of decolonization and deconstruction,
Of wilderness and wander,
Of feasts and ferocity,
Of goodness and grief,
We come to you today
With our whole selves.

God of our honest prayers and
More honest silences,
Open our eyes to see and
Our ears to hear and
Our hearts to understand
How you are already here with us.

Mother God, gather us as
A hen gathers her chicks

And let us catch our breath for
One hot second and remember
How you hold the whole world
In your kind, capable, wise hands,
Including us.

Spirit, when we cannot part the weeds
Of our own traditions and old languages,
When the old pathways of prayer feel choked
With briars and thorns,
Would you make a path in the wilderness
For us to find you in new ways, new words,
New practices, new permissions?
Would you meet us in the wilderness and
Set out a feast?
We are hungry and thirsty.

We are grateful for (mostly) every moment
That brought us here to
You.
Help us to sink down into your Love
To push our roots down into that marvellous Love.
And be planted within your power and grace
As we practice loving this world as you have
Loved this world.

May we laugh harder
Because we have learned

To let ourselves weep with you.
May we see and know and name Beauty
Because we have learned
To bring the ugliness to you.

Surprise us and startle us.
We're open to all the weird ways you want to
Speak—in us and to us and through us.

May we be Peacemakers,
Joy-bringers, Truth-tellers, Status-Quo-
    Disrupters,
Wanderers, Wonderers, and Misfits to our Time
    (because of
Resolute contentment),
Who never settle for the sit-down-and-shut-up life
But rise up in your
She-who-the-Son-sets-free-is-free-indeed
Birthright of freedom.

May we be the ones who come close to you
Because of our vulnerability and not
Because of our false certainties;
Teach us to lay down our masks and pretenses.
You tore down the veil between us and the Holy
    of Holies,
Keep our hands from rehanging that curtain.

Give us opportunities to practice mercy and
    courage
(This may backfire but we're feeling bold now.)
Call us to humility, confession, and repentance
    even when
Pride feels more comfortable and superior.
Teach us how to rest, how to abide, and how
To light candles and be satisfied.
Don't let us get away with divorcing our prayers
From our politics and policies and practices.
May we love our neighbors.

May we learn to sit with you,
In silence,
And know it is enough to know you
And be known by you
And know ourselves.

Teach us to pray, God, as you have always
Welcomed us to pray:
fully human, fully yours, fully held,
And fully loved.

We will tell you the truth of our lives
And of this world.
And we will listen to the truth you speak back
    to us

The truth of our belovedness,
Of your justice,
Of your faithfulness,
Of love.
And say
Let it be so,
Let it be in me.

Amen.

JOURNALING
PAGES

. . .

This sacred space is for you to dare to write your own prayers.

ACKNOWLEDGMENTS

...

I am (mostly) grateful that God never lets me get away with anything but continues to invite me into renewal and restoration. I'm never finished being made and re-made in response to Their unchanging Love. I love our talks, Jesus.

My deepest gratitude to the writers, leaders, ministers, and activists whose prayers grace these pages. In so many ways—both seen and unseen—you have taught me how to pray. You give so much more than permission, you light the way. Even if it damages the space-time continuum, let's plan on getting together, all of us, someday. Thank you to all of the readers who have asked me to talk more about prayer. I hope you don't regret it. And thanks to you, dear reader, for spending time with us in our prayer circle: it is a privilege and a joy to serve you.

Thank you to Ashley Hong, whose vision for this project was a source of energy and grace for me in a season when I needed both, and my deep thanks to the entire team at Convergent. Thanks to Rachelle Gardner, my agent and friend, who knew I needed something to put my hand to and stayed at my side. It has been a privilege to midwife this work into the world with you both.

I am grateful as always to my parents, my sister and her family, and dear friends—you're an answer to my prayers. Thank you to my husband and our four children: some of my deepest and most beloved prayers are at your bedside while you sleep or the beat-up supper table where we gather every night. I love to bear witness to your prayers, I hope you can always rest in mine.

And finally, my love and gratitude to Dan Evans and his two children, Amanda Opelt and family, Peter and Robin Held, and all of Rachel's family and friends. I hold Rachel and each one of you in my heart (I will forever) and, most days, this feels like prayer.

SARAH BESSEY is the author of the bestselling and critically acclaimed books *Miracles and Other Reasonable Things, Out of Sorts: Making Peace with an Evolving Faith,* and *Jesus Feminist.* She is also the co-creator of Evolving Faith with the late Rachel Held Evans and now serves as the co-leader for the community alongside Jeff Chu and their partner, Jim Chaffee.

Sarah is a sought-after speaker at churches, conferences, and universities all around the world. She also serves as President of the Board for Heartline Ministries in Haiti, which is committed to empowering Haitian families through complete maternal and infant health care, education, vocational training, and economic development.

Born and raised in western Canada, she now makes her home in Abbotsford, British Columbia, Canada, with her husband of nineteen years and their four children.

You can learn more at sarahbessey.com.

ABOUT THE TYPE

This book was set in Fournier, a typeface named for Pierre-Simon Fournier (1712–68), the youngest son of a French printing family. He started out engraving woodblocks and large capitals, then moved on to fonts of type. In 1736 he began his own foundry and made several important contributions in the field of type design; he is said to have cut 147 alphabets of his own creation. Fournier is probably best remembered as the designer of St. Augustine Ordinaire, a face that served as the model for the Monotype Corporation's Fournier, which was released in 1925.